TO SPREAD **SCRIPTURAL** HOLINESS

The New Methodism Summit once again provides a great service to the church, this time delivering a readable volume on the greatest Wesleyan distinctive of all. It reaches for the *grand depositum* to present a fresh vision for holiness of heart and life. A church that aligns with it will hear anew the call "to spread scriptural holiness over the land."

Brian Shelton
Dean, School of Christian Studies and Professor of Theology
Asbury University, Wilmore, KY

To Spread Scriptural Holiness is the heartbeat of Wesleyan scholars who seek to offer their theological reflection in service to the church. Readers will benefit from its biblical grounding, historical understanding, and practical wisdom as they seek to grow in Christlike character and love for the sake of the world.

Tammie Grimm
Associate Professor of Christian Discipleship and Practical Theology
Wesley Seminary, Indiana Wesleyan University, Marion, IN

What makes this work especially compelling is its breadth. It speaks not only to Methodists, but to Anglicans, Holiness, and Pentecostal believers, showing that the message of holiness transcends denominational boundaries and belongs to the gospel itself. Having stood among the nearly seventy scholars and church leaders who gathered in Alexandria, Virginia, I can attest first-hand to the careful collaboration, seasoned leadership, and thoughtful editing that produced a text both accessible and profound—a companion volume to *The Faith Once Delivered* and a vital resource for the church today.

John Mark Richardson
Executive Director, Wesleyan Holiness Connection
Western United States Regional Bishop in the
Church of God in Christ, Los Angeles, CA

Here is an engaging and invaluable resource that explores holy love from the new birth, the process of sanctification, and on to Christian perfection across the landscape of the personal, social, ethical, and political dimensions of a vibrant Christian discipleship so necessary for a hurting world today.

Kenneth J. Collins
Professor of Historical Theology and Wesley Studies
Director of the Wesleyan Studies Summer Seminar
Asbury Theological Seminary, Wilmore, KY

This text is a powerful witness to the efficacy of a comprehensive biblical approach to the doctrine of holiness. Understanding this doctrine as being rooted in the truth of Scripture allows Christ-followers to discuss and apply the principles of holiness to their lives in a way that is transformative for not only personal spiritual growth but also with a vision for the kingdom of God on earth as it is in heaven. By utilizing a diverse group of multi-disciplinary and multi-denominational scholars, the development of this text has produced language that readers will find easily accessible and applicable.

Grant Miller
Senior Pastor
Nashville First Church of the Nazarene, Nashville, TN

Here is a book for those alert pastors and laity whose focus in discipleship is the deep longing for a holy walk with God. *To Spread Scriptural Holiness* is a timely volume from the John Wesley Institute and a host of scholars and pastors from across the Wesleyan tradition. The distinctive character of sanctification-focused holiness theology, always at the center of the Methodist tradition, is presented clearly and concisely, from the doctrine of the Trinity to the preaching of sanctified concern for the needs of today's world. With the grand concern to "spread scriptural holiness over the land," this book will be a catalyst in the revival of Christian holiness for years to come.

Steven Hoskins
Professor of Church History
Trevecca Nazarene University, Nashville, TN

To Spread Scriptural Holiness presents a vibrant vision of the theological emphasis of the Wesleyan tradition. This articulation is the central message of Scripture. Namely, that by the power of the Holy Spirit, God can "sanctify us through and through." As Charles Wesley's work in his hymn "Love Divine," God longs to "fix in us [his] humble dwelling." This is a message our world desperately needs—a truth that speaks to the deepest longings of the human heart. This book consolidates this teaching in a way that is both theologically robust and timely for our day.

Andy Miller III
President and Associate Professor of Theology and Preaching
Wesley Biblical Seminary, Ridgeland, MS

This volume offers a vital and timely articulation of holiness, providing the broad Wesleyan tradition with a nuanced and faithful vision for understanding and embodying the life of sanctifying grace. It is an important work that calls us to clarity in our theology and integrity in how we live it.

Jonathan A. Powers
Associate Professor of Worship and Interim
Dean of the E. Stanley Jones School of Mission and Ministry
Asbury Theological Seminary, Wilmore, KY

Wesley's grand depositum has a twenty-first-century expression in this remarkable text. The Wesleyan tradition in all its expressions needs clarification on its central purpose for existence. The unique formation of a work born out of the combined training, wisdom, and mutual accountability of scholars has produced a true theology of holy love. The essence of the Holy One is the ground from which this instructive and challenging message arises. Holiness of heart and life, initial and entire, personal and social, ecclesial and societal, is unreservedly offered here for our day of witness. The fullness of the scriptural reality of the perfect love meets the reader from cover to cover.

M. William Ury
National Ambassador for Holiness
The Salvation Army USA, Raleigh, NC

To Spread Scriptural Holiness describes the full life possible through the Holy Spirit here and now. The good news of salvation through Jesus Christ does not stop with justification by faith; it begins and ends with grace, a grace that empowers believers to love God and love others. This book tells the rest of the story that is so often missing from theological descriptions of life in Christ. We are not living in this world, clinging to salvation by our fingernails, swayed by sin until our deaths. Rather, those who walk with the Holy Spirit are empowered now for the transformed life, a life of beauty and goodness that shines the light of Christ into a desperate world.

Suzanne Nicholson
Professor of New Testament
Asbury University, Wilmore, KY

TO SPREAD **SCRIPTURAL** HOLINESS

THEOLOGICAL, SOCIAL, AND MISSIONAL FOUNDATIONS FOR THE WESLEYAN MOVEMENT

EDITOR

Ryan N. Danker

Printed in the United States of America

Cover layout by Nate Farro
Page layout by PerfecType, Nashville, Tennessee

To spread scriptural holiness : theological, social, and missional foundations for the Wesleyan Movement / Ryan N. Danker, general editor. – Franklin, Tennessee : Seedbed Publishing, ©2026.

pages ; cm.

ISBN 9798888001813 (paperback)
ISBN 9798888001820 (ePub)
ISBN 9798888001837 (uPDF)
OCLC 1564425579

1. Holiness--Christianity. 2. Holiness--Biblical teaching. 3. Christian life--Methodist authors. 4. Conduct of life--Religious aspects--Christianity. 5. Methodist Church--Doctrines. 6. Methodism--Doctrines. I. Title. II. Danker, Ryan Nicholas, 1979- editor.

BT767.T67 2026 2026932717

SEEDBED PUBLISHING
Franklin, Tennessee
seedbed.com

CONTENTS

SIGNATORIES

Dr. Reggie Abraham
United Theological Seminary
International Fellowship of
Christian Assemblies (Pentecostal)

Dr. Kevin Anderson
Asbury University
Anglican Church in North
America

Dr. Bill T. Arnold
Asbury Theological Seminary
Global Methodist Church

Dr. Pete Bellini
United Theological Seminary
Global Methodist Church

Dr. Chris Bounds
Asbury Theological Seminary
United Methodist Church

Rev. Keith Boyette
Global Methodist Church

Dr. Cheryl Bridges Johns
United Theological Seminary
International Pentecostal Holiness
Church

Dr. Steve Bruns
Asbury Theological Seminary
Free Methodist Church

Dr. Friedemann Burkhardt
Internationale Hochschule
Liebenzell
Global Methodist Church

Dr. Julianne Burnett
Asbury University
Global Methodist Church

Dr. Constance Cherry
Robert E. Webber Institute for
Worship Studies
Global Methodist Church

Dr. Joel Chopp
Asbury Theological Seminary
Anglican Church in North America

Dr. Rachel Coleman
Indiana Wesleyan University
Global Methodist Church

Dr. Dale Coulter
Pentecostal Theological Seminary
Church of God, Cleveland, TN

Dr. Bruce Cromwell
Superintendent, Central Region Conference
Free Methodist Church

Dr. Ryan Danker
The John Wesley Institute
The Church of England/The Episcopal Church, USA

Dr. Lane Davis
Christian Theological Seminary
United Methodist Church

Dr. Jim Fitzgerald
Southern Nazarene University
Church of the Nazarene

Dr. Sègbégnon Mathieu Gnonhossou
Seattle Pacific University
Free Methodist Church

Dr. Tammie Grimm
Indiana Wesleyan University
United Methodist Church

Dr. Charles Harrell
Global Methodist Church

Dr. Robert Haynes
World Methodist Evangelism
The Wesleyan Church

Dr. Madeline Henners
United Theological Seminary
Global Methodist Church

Dr. Isaac Hopper
Global Methodist Church

Dr. Steven Hoskins
Trevecca Nazarene University
Church of the Nazarene

Dr. Jack Jackson
Foundation for Evangelism
United Methodist Church

Bishop Scott Jones
Global Methodist Church

Dr. Abson Joseph
Bethel University
The Wesleyan Church

Dr. Scott Kisker
Asbury Theological Seminary
Global Methodist Church

Dr. Doug Koskela
Seattle Pacific University
Free Methodist Church

Dr. Bill Kostlevy
Asbury Theological Seminary
Church of the Brethren

Dr. Jessica LaGrone
Asbury Theological Seminary
Global Methodist Church

Dr. Jackson Lashier
Southwestern College
United Methodist Church

Bishop Mike Lowry
Global Methodist Church

Dr. Kenneth Loyer
Spry Church
Independent

Dr. Tesia Mallory
Asbury Theological Seminary
Global Methodist Church

Dr. Andy Miller
Wesley Biblical Seminary
Global Methodist Church

Dr. Grant Miller
Northwest Nazarene University
Church of the Nazarene

Dr. Stacy Minger
Asbury Theological Seminary
United Methodist Church

Dr. Wendy Mohler-Seib
Friends University
Global Methodist Church

Dr. Joy J. Moore
Northern Seminary
United Methodist Church

Dr. Suzanne Nicholson
Asbury University
Global Methodist Church

Dr. Luther Oconer
Asbury Theological Seminary
Global Methodist Church

Dr. Matt O'Reilly
Christ Church
Global Methodist Church

Dr. John Oswalt
Asbury Theological Seminary
Free Methodist Church

Dr. Michael Pasquarello
Beeson Divinity School
United Methodist Church

Dr. Jonathan Powers
Asbury Theological Seminary
Anglican Church in North America

Dr. Stephen Rankin
Spiritual Maturity Project
United Methodist Church

Dr. Ruth Anne Reese
Asbury Theological Seminary
Anglican Church in North America

Dr. Kimberly Reisman
World Methodist Evangelism
United Methodist Church

Bishop John Mark Richardson
Wesleyan Holiness Connection
Church of God in Christ

Dr. Brian Russell
Asbury Theological Seminary
United Methodist Church

Dr. Elvin Sadler
United Theological Seminary
African Methodist Episcopal Church Zion

Dr. Joel Scandrett
Trinity Anglican Seminary
Anglican Church in North America

Dr. Brian Shelton
Asbury University
Anglican Church in North America

Dr. Warren Smith
The Divinity School, Duke University
Attends St. Thomas More Catholic Church, Chapel Hill

Dr. Phil Tallon
Houston Christian University
Global Methodist Church

Dr. Chappell Temple
Global Methodist Church

Dr. James Thobaben
Asbury Theological Seminary
Global Methodist Church

Dr. Andrew Thompson
First Methodist Church, Tulsa
Independent

Dr. Thomas Tumblin
Asbury Theological Seminary
Global Methodist Church

Dr. Bill Ury
The Salvation Army

Dr. Jerome Van Kuiken
Oklahoma Wesleyan University
The Wesleyan Church

Dr. Joy Vaughan
Asbury University
Global Methodist Church

Dr. David Watson
Asbury Theological Seminary
Global Methodist Church

Dr. Kevin Watson
Asbury Theological Seminary
Global Methodist Church

Dr. Mike Weaver
Bradley Study Center
Global Methodist Church

Dr. Brian Yeich
Wesley Biblical Seminary
Global Methodist Church

INTRODUCTION

1. In January of 2024, nearly seventy scholars and church leaders from fifteen different Wesleyan and Anglican denominations gathered in Alexandria, Virginia, to craft a document on holiness of heart and life. The book that you have now before you is the direct result of that three-day gathering called The Next Methodism II: Holiness. The purpose of the book is to shape and form contemporary Wesleyan witness on this vital doctrinal teaching, with the hope that it will be both preached and experienced in its transforming power.

2. Early Methodism was a movement driven by the firm belief that God's grace is more powerful than the brokenness of the human situation. In fact, John and Charles Wesley, their fellow clergy associates, and the army of lay preachers that joined the movement, all believed that the only reason that God had raised up the Methodists was to preach this doctrine of wholeness and freedom. John Wesley made the claim numerous times throughout his ministry, but explicitly when he wrote: "This doctrine is the grand depositum which God has lodged with the people called Methodists; and for the sake of propagating this chiefly He appeared to have raised us up" (Letter to Robert Carr Brackenbury, Sept. 15, 1790).

3. The doctrine of holiness of heart and life encompasses the entire Christian life. It begins with God and his work to call us into a saving relationship

through his Son, Jesus Christ. The end, or goal, of that call is wholeness, even in this life. God gives us new life in Christ by justifying us through faith, pardoning us of all that is past, and giving us new birth by the Spirit. In the sermon, "The New Birth," Wesley preached that God is "continually breathing, as it were, upon the soul," opening to believers the joy of intimate fellowship with God and others. The goal of this new life in Christ has different names, including: *full salvation, perfect love, entire sanctification, Christian perfection, holiness of heart and life*. At its core, though, sanctification is the transformation of our hearts to love God supremely and to love our neighbors—to be filled with holy love.

4. Throughout the history of Methodism, the doctrine of holiness of heart and life has been preached and different emphases placed on certain aspects of the doctrine. John Wesley's original vision of Christlikeness made possible by new birth, growth in grace, and the freedom of holy love has sometimes been misunderstood. Wesley taught that perfection is best understood as wholeness, or a life lived as Christ did. Some have mistakenly thought that he was promoting a static form of sinless perfection. This was not his message. He taught that we must rely on the means of grace, especially Holy Communion, as we grow in Christlikeness. At the heart of holiness is a dynamic relationship with the only One who is truly holy. Others mistakenly believed that we didn't need any sort of communal formation. Wesley taught that sanctification is both a process of growth and an instantaneous moment of transformation (followed by more growth). Others focused so heavily on the process that they never expected transformation in this life, or so much on the instantaneous that they confused the new birth with entire sanctification. Still others focused so much on the dos and don'ts of a holy life that it became a legalistic trap rather than freedom found in holy love. But the original vision that Wesley taught remains, and it is both scripturally true and a powerful witness of God's work in the world.

5. And this message is for all. If you've read the words *Methodist* or *Wesleyan* in a denominational sense, that's not the way the terms are used in this book. Keep in mind that the early Methodists were almost all Anglicans. And later,

the Wesleyan movement would include different groups who might be called Methodist, Holiness, or Pentecostal. The summit that gathered in January 2024 to write this work reflected the broad diversity of the Wesleyan movement just described—Anglican, Methodist, Holiness, and Pentecostal—with various denominational groups represented within each category. Both institutional and church affiliation has been provided in the list of signatories to show this diversity. Ultimately, the message of holiness doesn't belong to a denomination or a movement, but rather to the gospel. In this book we aim to proclaim nothing but the fullness of the gospel of Jesus Christ, and to describe the life of perfect love available in him.

6. The work completed during the initial summit of 2024 was done by groups who focused on the different parts of the text before you. Each group had seasoned and thoughtful leadership. A committee of well-established scholars and church leaders oversaw the summit itself. Following the initial gathering, the texts from the groups were gathered and a team of editors set to work to give the document coherence, to make sure it used accessible language, and to add Scripture verses or quotes from other sources to augment the text. I want to thank Wendy Mohler-Seib, Suzanne Nicholson, Jonathan Powers, and Joel Scandrett for joining me in the editing process. The book that you have in front of you, however, is essentially the work of the summit participants.

7. Throughout the work, you will find references to Scripture, the church fathers, the Wesley brothers, and other notable figures in church history. The primary aim was to be scriptural, and with that primary aim in mind, we engaged the larger tradition of the Church and the specific gifts of the Wesleyan movement.

8. Summit participants were also encouraged to reference *The Faith Once Delivered: A Wesleyan Witness to Christian Orthodoxy* (Seedbed, 2024), the work of the first summit hosted by the John Wesley Institute in 2022. References to *The Faith Once Delivered* are marked as *TFOD* with a corresponding paragraph number. Paragraph numbers have also been provided in this text for similar reference. The hope is that both *TFOD* and now *To Spread*

Scriptural Holiness (*TSSH*) can be used as formative companion volumes throughout the Wesleyan world and beyond.

9. The message of holiness is nothing less than the witness of Scripture, of the early Church, and as Wesley himself would add, of the Church of England. Christ invites all into a dynamic, grace-empowered, and transforming relationship. And as we walk with him and learn his ways, the result is freedom. It is that freedom that this text hopes not just to describe but to proclaim, to engage the original mission of Methodism, "to reform the nation, and in particular the Church, to spread scriptural holiness over the land" (John Wesley, "'Large' Minutes of 1763").

Ryan N. Danker
Washington, DC

CHAPTER I

The Holy Trinity: Ground of Holiness

Beginning with God

10. The topic of this book is holiness. But we can't talk about holiness without first talking about God. As Christians, we begin with God. He is the very definition of holiness. His defining character is holiness. In this way, he is unique from all created things. This uniqueness is the basic understanding of what it means to be "God" in the Bible. But what does it mean to say that God's very character is holiness? The holiness of God is mystery, making his core essence beyond the grasp of the human mind. It is also beauty itself, making him utterly ravishing. The psalmist wrote about this beauty when he wrote that he longed to "live in the house of the LORD all the days of my life, to behold the beauty of the LORD" (Ps. 27:4). God's holiness is morally convicting; no one who encounters him in his holiness can see themselves as anything but filthy. All of God's other attributes can be understood as aspects of his holiness. It is because he is holy, transcending all else, that he can only be understood as one.

11. It is because God is holy that no created thing can adequately represent him, no analogy can be used to describe God because it would fail to grasp him. We often sing of this in the words of the famous hymn, "Holy, Holy, Holy! Lord God Almighty," where the author, Reginald Heber, wrote:

> Holy, holy, holy! Though the darkness hide Thee,
> though the eye of sinful man Thy glory may not see,
> only Thou art holy; there is none beside Thee,
> perfect in pow'r, in love and purity.

This otherness, God's uniqueness, applies also to his character, his name. There is no other being like him. His character is unlike that of any other. His name is, above all, self-giving and other-oriented love. But he is also true—absolutely dependable; he is purity—he is one in all his dealings; he is good—consistently and always intending the best for his creatures; he is just—maintaining that divine order by which alone humans can flourish; and he is right—everything he does is for the proper end. His very character is holy.

12. This holy character is an expression of the inner life of the Trinity. In the prophet Isaiah's vision, the angels spoke of this inner life when they cried aloud before God, "Holy, holy, holy" (Isa. 6:3), the same text that inspired Heber's hymn. God is the three-times Holy One. The three persons of the Trinity manifest these qualities, this holiness, in their relation to one another. Holiness is not just an attribute of one person of the Trinity—it belongs to the essence of God; the Father is holy, the Son is holy, and the Spirit is holy.

13. Holiness also characterizes the relationship of the Father, the Son, and the Spirit in their own perfect life together. It is to share the joy of this kind of holy and perfect life that creation, culminating in human beings, was brought into being (2 Peter 1:4). As bearers of the Image of God, humans were intended to "be holy" as he is holy, walking in unbroken fellowship with the triune One (Lev. 11:44; 19:2). When humans fell, the program of salvation was immediately launched to restore us to this true fellowship, to remove all of the obstacles that humanity, and the creation, now faced. Salvation restores our original purpose.

Divine Holiness in Creation

14. The creation speaks of God's holiness. He displays it to us in all of his visible works. He created everything that is, and he created it out of nothing (Gen. 1:1; Heb. 11:3; Isa. 45:18; *TFOD*, ¶60). We can see this clearly in the creation story of Genesis 1 where a pattern emerges in the text, "And God said" and it is so—whether light, animals, or humanity itself. And while God reveals his holiness in his creation, he and the creation are not the same. He is eternal, yet creation is bound by time. God does not change, yet all created

things do. Who he is, his character, is not impacted by his interactions with the creation. Creatures, however, undergo suffering and loss, but God exists entirely in and of himself. Our existence depends on God at every moment. God is simple, not made up of parts or pieces; creation is complex, composed of separable elements and subject to decomposition. God is perfectly and necessarily good; creatures are only good insofar as they participate in his goodness, and they can fall away from it (*TFOD*, ¶¶15–19).

15. In all of these ways God shows us that he transcends what he created and that he is separate from it. He is not a part of it. And because God is holy, he is also separate from all that is morally evil. Thus, God's holiness includes his moral perfection. But it's also more than that. This is expressed well by John Wesley in his notes on the book of Revelation:

> When God is termed holy, it denotes that excellence which is altogether peculiar to himself; and the glory flowing from all his attributes conjoined, . . . whereby he is, and eternally remains, in an incomprehensible manner, separate and at a distance, not only from all that is impure, but likewise all that is created. (*Explanatory Notes Upon the New Testament*; Rev. 4:8)

16. Even the way that God created humanity revealed his holiness. He created us in his Image (Gen. 1:26–27; *TFOD*, ¶¶67–76). When he did so, he created humanity "straightforward" (Eccl. 7:29), which means that humans were created in a right relationship with God. In other words, they were holy (Eph. 4:24). Wesley taught a threefold picture of what it means for humanity to be created in the Image of God. This included: the natural image, in which humans were created with a spiritual nature and immortal soul, capable of a relationship with God; the political image, in which humans were created to be stewards of creation, relating to nature itself and other creatures; and, finally, the moral image, in which humanity was created to live according to God's will in holy love, in moral purity, and in loving relationship with God and others (John Wesley, "On the Image of God"; *TFOD*, ¶¶72–74).

Divine Holiness and Love

17. But we can't speak of God's holiness apart from his love. His holiness is inseparable from it. This is seen in John's claim that "God is love" (1 John 4:8, 16). It is not said that he loves, as an action, but that he *is* love, in his essence. The key terms here are the Hebrew word *hesed* and the Greek word *agape*. These words have virtually the same meaning. That meaning is one of self-giving, other-oriented, sacrificial love. It is not something someone feels, but something that one does; it is to choose the best for another at whatever cost to oneself. God is in himself eternally characterized by this behavior. It is characteristic of the Trinity: the Father eternally loves the Son (John 17:24) and willingly allows the Son to represent him in the world; the Son eternally loves the Father and is delighted to do nothing but what the Father directs; the Spirit eternally loves the Father and the Son and delights to reveal them. The Trinity does not simply embody this behavior but is its very origin and source.

18. So when Jesus explains what it means to live in the kingdom of heaven (Matt. 5–7), he first shows that the central principle of God's law, his instructions for life, is love (5:21–48). It is not a question of narrowly fulfilling the command not to murder; it is whether we hold people in contempt, murdering them in our hearts. Do we value others, or do we simply view them as competitors (vv. 21–26)? Jesus ends this part of the Sermon on the Mount with verses 38–48, where he shows that God's love is perfect, complete. It does not need the love of others for it to be extended in the first place, nor does it need the love of others for it to be continued. So, when Jesus calls humans to "be perfect, therefore, as your heavenly Father is perfect" (v. 48), he is not demanding that we show flawless performance in all areas of life. Rather, he is—astoundingly—offering us the possibility of sharing in the same kind of love that God himself demonstrates: a love that is complete (perfect) in itself. Essentially, he is calling us to share the holy character of God. This is what John points to when he speaks of "perfect love" (1 John 4:18). He is not talking about flawless performance. Instead, he is speaking about the God-given ability to choose the best for others regardless of their attitude to

us. Having experienced this divine gift, we are assured that we are truly the children of God (vv. 12–13).

19. Such love as this epitomizes God's otherness. The only loves the world knows are *storge*, the passion of a mother animal to protect her offspring; *phileo*, affection for a friend; or *eros*, attraction to, and appreciation for, one who will meet one's needs. All of these tend to be self-oriented, and that condition is magnified in the behavior of the false gods. They are not qualified to be called holy, other, because they only live to promote themselves; they are just humans written large. The God of the Bible, however, is truly holy because *he is in himself self-giving love.*

20. There is a sense in which Genesis 17:1–2, where God renews his promise to Abram, points to Matthew 5:48 in Jesus's Sermon on the Mount. After the tragic circumstances surrounding the birth of Ishmael, when Abram tried to fulfill God's promises in his own power, thirteen years passed. God addressed Abram again, renewing the promises that he had made. He began by giving the instruction or promise: "I am God Almighty; walk before me, and be blameless" (Gen. 17:1b). The word translated as "blameless" is *tammim*, which is the same word used to describe an acceptable sacrificial animal, one that is whole, complete, all that a sacrificial animal should be. This is what God is offering Abram. He, the One in whom all power resides, is offering a life of fellowship with himself (a "walk"), the result of which will be Abram becoming all he was ever meant to be, a person living out a divinely initiated, unconditional love for God and other humans—holiness. So, "You shall be holy, for I am holy" (Lev. 11:45b), is also to say, "You shall give yourselves away in love, because I, the source of all being, give myself in love."

Holiness and Evil

21. God's holiness is contrary to evil. When God created, he created everything good (Gen. 1:31; 1 Tim. 4:4). So if everything created is good, Christian tradition recognizes that evil is not actually a created thing or a substance.

It's not a "thing" (Augustine, *Confessions*; Aquinas, *On Evil*). Instead, evil is an absence of good in the same way that darkness is the absence of light. The tragedy of human sin is that it causes us to turn away from God, the source of all goodness, so that our hearts and wills are curved in on ourselves and bent toward sin. The good that is meant to be there is absent because of sin. And because life is a gift of God, having been cut off from the life of the soul through sin, death is the inevitable result.

22. The origin of moral evil is not found in God. Sin does not originate with him (Ps. 5:4; 1 John 1:5; 2:16; Augustine, *Eighty-Three Different Questions*). The possibility of sin is in the changeable wills of his weak creatures, those who misuse their will and fall for temptation. This took place first with Satan, and then through the temptation by Satan of Adam and Eve (Rom. 5:19; John Wesley, "The End of Christ's Coming"). But sin occurs under God's sovereign rule and reign; for his own holy purposes, God permits sin, and in his mercy provides a means of redemption and freedom from sin.

23. If a sharing in the holy character of God is the goal of human existence, why is this not the common experience of the human race? It is because of the disposition of all of the descendants of Adam and Eve to deny the implication of God's holiness; namely, that humans cannot be equal to God (Gen. 3:5). In the Old Testament when people encountered God, they expressed wonder afterward that they were still alive (e.g., Gen. 16:13). Yet, even with experiences like that we continue to try to remove God from his rightful place in the world and in our lives. This is the disposition of sin, and while this disposition of sin may lead to acts of immorality, it does not do so necessarily. The disposition is just as likely to instill in us a self-righteous morality born of pride (Isa. 65:5). It is this disposition to pride that is particularly counter to holiness. In fact, pride and holiness cannot exist together: "For thus says the high and lofty one who inhabits eternity, whose name is Holy: I dwell in the high and holy place, and also with those who are contrite and humble in spirit, to revive the spirit of the humble, and to revive the heart of the contrite" (Isa. 57:15).

The Work of the Son in Sanctification

24. The work of the Son in sanctification builds upon, restores, and perfects his original work in creation. Although through him the world came into being and is sustained, the world has rebelled against its Creator (John 1:3–4; Col. 1:15–17; Heb. 1:2–3). Yet even as the world rebelled, God promised a Savior (Gen. 3:15) and called together a covenant people to prepare the way for his coming. Across Israel's history God raised up prophets, priests, and kings. Prophets proclaimed God's holiness through inspired words and miraculous deeds, rebuking the people's bondage and sin and calling them to total devotion to God. Priests mediated between God, who is holy, and a sinful people by offering sacrifices, interceding in prayer, and teaching reverence for God. Kings were empowered by God's Spirit to enact justice, to stand up against Israel's enemies, and to build or restore God's temple. Yet as we can see in the pages of the Old Testament, the covenant people repeatedly rejected God and his representatives, while those representatives themselves often failed to uphold their calling. False prophets, corrupt priests, and idolatrous and unjust kings compounded Israel's rebellion against God, and so Israel failed in its mission to embody divine holiness in such a way as to be a light to the nations.

25. In the tension between Israel's calling and its continued rebellion, God the Father sent his only Son in the fullness of time to fulfill his promised purpose. John states this clearly in the beginning ofhis Gospel. "The Word became flesh" (John 1:14) when—by the power of the Holy Spirit—God the Son joined himself to a full human nature in the Virgin Mary's womb. Charles Wesley described this poetically in the hymn "Let Earth and Heaven Combine" when he wrote: "Our God contracted to a span, incomprehensibly made man."

26. At his birth, both Jewish shepherds and Gentile sages greeted him as the heaven-attested king of Israel (Luke 2:8–16; Matt. 2:1–11). When Jesus was circumcised as a child and dedicated at the temple in accordance with the law (Luke 2:21–38), Simeon the prophet hailed him as a holy "light for revelation to the Gentiles and for glory to your people Israel" (v. 32).

27. At the beginning of his ministry, Jesus submitted to a baptism of repentance. He did so not because he was sinful and needed to be cleansed like we do, but "to fulfill all righteousness" (Matt. 3:15). He did this to step into the place of the sinners, the ones he came to save. God the Father confirmed Jesus's holy identity and mission by publicly naming him "my Son" and sending the Holy Spirit upon him (vv. 16–17). In this way, Jesus's baptism and reception of the Spirit offer a model for the Church's imitation (Cyril of Alexandria, *Adv. Nestorium*). Led by the Spirit, Jesus entered into testing in the desert. Like Adam and Eve in the garden and Israel itself in the desert, he experienced temptation, but unlike them he remained faithful and sinless. The holy Image of God that humanity defiled in Eden and that Israel failed to reflect now found its perfect fulfillment in Jesus Christ, the "Second Adam from above" (Charles Wesley, "Hark! the Herald Angels Sing") and "Israel's strength and consolation" (Charles Wesley, "Come, Thou Long-Expected Jesus").

28. After passing through baptism and temptation, Jesus carried out his public ministry. He cast out unclean spirits, who confessed him as "the Holy One of God" (Mark 1:24). His contagious holiness healed the sick, made the blind to see, cleansed the lepers, and raised the dead. He fellowshipped with sinners and forgave their sins. He debated hypocritical religious leaders and exposed their sins. He called his disciples to be pure in heart, to take up their cross, to seek first God's kingdom, and to be perfect in love like their heavenly Father (Matt. 5:8, 48; 6:33; 16:24). He himself set the pattern for a holy life, so that we who follow him are invited to have "all the mind which was in Christ, enabling us to walk as Christ walked" (John Wesley, *A Plain Account of Christian Perfection*; see "Christian Perfection").

29. Jesus's public ministry culminated in his triumphal entry in Jerusalem as the King who came bringing salvation. He confronted corruption in the temple and warned of God's impending judgment upon it. Then he gathered his disciples to celebrate the establishment of a new covenant, one that would be based in his own broken body and outpoured blood, and consequently, one that would be marked by self-giving love and the presence of the Holy Spirit (Matt. 26:26–28; John 13–16). Jesus then withdrew to a garden where, like

Adam in Eden once more, he faced the choice of obedience or disobedience to God's will. But unlike Adam, he chose God's way—at the cost of his very life. Betrayed and crucified, he died as a holy sacrifice for the sin of the whole world "in order to sanctify the people by his own blood" (Heb. 13:12). On the cross, Christ displayed the divine holiness as perfect love for sinners and perfect judgment on sin (Rom. 3:25–26; 5:8; 1 John 4:9–12). Charles Wesley described this sacrifice for sin in one of his hymns, "O Love Divine, What Hast Thou Done":

> O Love divine, what hast Thou done!
> Th'immortal God hath died for me!
> The Father's co-eternal Son
> bore all my sins upon the tree.
> Th'immortal God for me hath died:
> my Lord, my Love, is crucified!

30. But his death was not the end. Jesus rose again from the dead, confirming his claim to be the Son of God and conquering sin, death, and the devil (1 Cor. 15; Col. 2:14–15). As the perfect High Priest, he ascended into heaven to intercede for us on the basis of his once-for-all sacrifice (Rom. 8:34; Heb. 7:25; 1 John 2:1). As the victorious King and prophetic Word, he pours out his Holy Spirit on the Church so as to "rule in all our hearts alone" (Charles Wesley, "Come, Thou Long-Expected Jesus") and guide us into all truth (John 16:12–15). John Wesley describes Christ's continuing role in our sanctification:

> The holiest of men still need Christ as their Prophet, as "the light of the world." For he does not give them light but from moment to moment; the instant he withdraws, all is darkness. They still need Christ as their King. For God does not give them a stock of holiness. But unless they received a supply every moment, nothing but unholiness would remain. They still need Christ as their Priest, to make atonement for their holy things. Even perfect holiness is acceptable to God only through Jesus Christ. (*A Plain Account of Christian Perfection*)

And he will come again with glory to finalize his victory over the enemies of God and fully renew his creation in holiness (1 Cor. 15; Rev. 21–22).

The Work of the Spirit in Sanctification

31. In one of John Wesley's most important works, "A Letter to a Roman Catholic," he describes the many beliefs that Christians share, including belief in the Holy Spirit:

> I believe the infinite and eternal Spirit of God, equal with the Father and the Son, to be not only perfectly holy in himself, but the immediate cause of all holiness in us; enlightening our understandings, rectifying our wills and affections, renewing our natures, uniting our persons to Christ, assuring us of the adoption of sons, leading us in our actions; purifying and sanctifying our souls and bodies, to a full and eternal enjoyment of God.

Wesley's description of the Spirit's sanctifying work includes a number of themes. We can see in the description: the relationship between the work of Christ and the Holy Spirit, the Spirit's regenerating (i.e., bringing to life) work in the sacrament of baptism, the new birth offered to the believer, the sanctification and nurturing of the Church through Holy Communion and the means of grace, and the gifts of the Spirit itself resulting in love, joy, peace, etc., by which the Church bears witness to Christ in order to bring the world to him.

32. The work of Christ and the work of the Spirit are inseparable because the Spirit completes the work of Christ begun in his incarnation. The Virgin Mary conceived Jesus through the overshadowing of the Spirit. His cousin, John the Baptist, promised that Jesus would baptize his followers with the Spirit and with fire (Matt. 3:11; Luke 3:16). Charles Wesley wrote about this prophecy in his hymn "Jesus, Thine All-Victorious Love":

> Jesus, Thine all-victorious love
> shed in my heart abroad;
> then shall my feet no longer rove,
> rooted and fixed in God. . . .

Refining fire, go through my heart,
illuminate my soul;
scatter Thy life through every part,
and sanctify the whole.

33. At the beginning of Jesus's public ministry, the Holy Spirit anoints him at his baptism. We receive the same gift at our baptism now. Jesus begins his ministry with this anointing and announces the coming kingdom of God and freedom to captive humanity (Luke 4:18; Isa. 11:2; 61:1). He told his disciples, "I came that you might have life and have it abundantly" (John 10:10, paraphrased). This is the life offered by the Spirit. The fourth-century bishop Athanasius described the Spirit as the "living water" that Christ offers the woman at the well—"living water that wells up into eternal life" ("Letter to Serapion"; John 4:14; 7:38). Jesus prayed to the Father that he would send the Spirit of truth (John 17:17) to convince the world of the reality of sin, to bear witness to the hope of forgiveness, and to sanctify them in his word and truth (16:7–11). It was the Spirit of holiness who raised Jesus from the dead. Therefore, after his resurrection, Jesus breathed the Holy Spirit onto the disciples—just as God breathed life into the first Adam—that they might know that the Spirit at work in them is Christ's own Spirit (John 20:22). The new life Jesus offers through the Holy Spirt is the life of holiness for those who walk in the Spirit.

34. The promised gift of the Holy Spirit in baptism is not just for us as individuals only but for us as the one body of Christ. Paul explains that our baptism is a participation in Christ's death and resurrection. He describes how we are plunged into Christ's death in the waters of baptism and raised to the new life of grace. This unites us with the faithful everywhere and throughout all time, the body of Christ. Sin is put to death that we might be freed from captivity to it and to walk in newness of life. This life is a life of holiness, made possible by Christ's Spirit who dwells in us (Rom. 6:8).

35. Repentance marks the beginning of this new life. And it is the Spirit that makes repentance possible. The early Christian teacher Origen explained the importance of repentance as a precondition for new life in his interpretation

of Jesus's parable of the wine and the wineskins (Mark 2:22). The Spirit is the new wine that Jesus gives, but which cannot be contained within old wineskins. The wineskins are an image of the old life or former life in the world that does not recognize the authority and lordship of Christ (Origen of Alexandria, *On First Principles*). Charles Wesley describes the liberation of the justifying and sanctifying work of grace to forgive sin and release us from its power in his hymn, "And Can It Be That I Should Gain":

> Long my imprisoned spirit lay,
> fast bound in sin and nature's night;
> Thine eye diffused a quick'ning ray;
> I woke, the dungeon flamed with light;
> my chains fell off, my heart was free,
> I rose, went forth and followed Thee.

36. In his sermon, "The Scripture Way of Salvation," John Wesley describes the Spirit's role in moving us along the journey of the new life of holiness:

> And at the same time that we are justified, yea, in that very moment, sanctification begins. In that instant we are born again, born from above, born of the Spirit: there is a real as well as a relative change. We are inwardly renewed by the power of God. We feel "the love of God shed abroad in our hearts by the Holy Ghost which is given unto us." [see Rom. 5:5]

Wesley here says that sanctification begins the moment that we are justified; our wholeness begins with our pardon. In response to God's forgiveness, the Spirit awakens in us both gratitude and a love for God. Yet Wesley held that the impulse of sin remained in the heart but, by the power of the Spirit, does not reign. For "We are enabled by the Spirit to mortify the deeds of the body of our evil nature" ("Scripture Way of Salvation," see Rom. 8:13). Therefore, there was the need for continued growth in grace that would bring the believer to "entire sanctification" (i.e., the perfect love of God and neighbor). "It is love excluding sin; love filling the heart, taking up the whole capacity of the soul" ("Scripture Way of Salvation").

37. Love of God and neighbor, both of them gifts of the Spirit, is the essential mark of the restored Image of God in the individual believer and the whole community of faith. Without this restoration, there is no true holiness. Drawing on Romans 5:5 that speaks of "the love of God poured into our hearts by the Spirit who is given to us," Augustine of Hippo explained that the Holy Spirit is able to unite us to God and to each other because the Spirit is the Father's love for the Son and the Son's love for the Father (*On the Trinity*). So in this way, the Spirit calls the Church to unity, bearing witness to the unity of the Trinity. This unity of love is the fruit of the believer's participation in what Paul called "the communion of the Holy Spirit" (2 Cor. 13:13).

38. Christ's "gift" of the Spirit (2 Tim. 1:6) is nothing less than the Spirit's indwelling the heart of believers. John Wesley recognized that the disciples at Pentecost were filled with the Spirit that included both sanctifying grace and miraculous gifts or charisms. Early Methodists received both. Likewise, we should be filled with the holiness and power of the Spirit (*Explanatory Notes Upon the New Testament*; Acts 1:5; 8:15). In this indwelt community, different gifts are given to different people for the building up of the whole body in holy love.

39. In line with Church teaching, John Wesley believed that we encounter Christ in Holy Communion. This is the work of the Spirit. And in this encounter, we are changed. We are made like him. Charles Wesley describes the Spirit's mysterious work in the Lord's Supper in "O The Depth of Love Divine":

> O the depth of love divine,
> th'unfathomable grace!
> Who shall say how bread and wine
> God into us conveys?
> How the bread his flesh imparts,
> how the wine transmits His blood,
> Fills His faithful people's hearts
> with all the life of God!

40. Holy Communion is the chief means of grace and will be discussed in greater detail in chapter 4 of this book. But the means of grace are vital to the journey of holiness. *The Faith Once Delivered* defines means of grace as "a channel by which God communicates grace: the power of the Holy Spirit" (¶155). These include works of piety, such as prayer and meditating on Scripture, and works of mercy, such as visiting the sick (see *TFOD*, ¶¶157–91). In the means of grace, the believer encounters the grace offered by the Spirit. Since grace is the power of God communicated by his very presence, the means of grace serve as reliable ways through which God works in us. It is the Spirit who calls the Christian to meet him in the means of grace, but the Christian must also live a disciplined life, one that opens us to the sanctifying movement of the Spirit.

41. The Spirit's work in us now is preparation for the absolute holiness of the new creation. Christ, in his death and resurrection, launched the new creation, but it will only be brought to completion when he returns. John Wesley explained this in his sermon "The New Creation":

> Hence will arise an unmixed state of holiness and happiness far superior to that which Adam enjoyed in paradise. . . . [T]here will be no more sin. And to crown all, there will be a deep, an intimate, an uninterrupted union with God; a constant communion with the Father and his Son Jesus Christ, through the Spirit; a continual enjoyment of the Three-One God, and of all the creatures in him!

This is the ultimate hope that we have, a true gift of wholeness given to us by God: Father, Son, and Holy Spirit.

CHAPTER 2

Scriptural Holiness: Command and Promise

The General Tenor of Scripture

42. John Wesley famously referred to himself as "a man of one book." He didn't mean that he only read one book, but that one book—the Bible—was more important to him than any other. Only one book can show us how to be saved. For Wesley, being saved is not simply going to heaven (though that is part of it), but the good life that God shows us in Scripture, living as the people we were created to be. The world promises us many versions of the good life, but only one way—God's way—is truly good. The good life is not a life without suffering or hardship. It is a life lived in agreement with the will of God as revealed in Scripture. All of Wesley's preaching and teaching had the goal of leading people into this good life. Scripture talks about the good life in a variety of ways, using a wide range of vocabulary and images, including *blessedness, salvation,* the *divine life,* and *holiness.*

43. Wesley believed that the primary function of Scripture is to lead us into the fullness of salvation, both by mediating God's presence to us and teaching us how to be saved. For Wesley, commands found in Scripture are "covered promises." He means by this that God empowers us to fulfill his commandments. When we hear the command to "be holy" in Scripture, it is spoken in the voice of the God who is present in the Scriptures and who promises to make us holy. He doesn't command without also empowering.

44. Scripture is more than a repository of information. It is a pathway into the life of God whereby we become participants of the divine nature. It is the terrain of divine encounter. Wesley understood Scripture as a means of grace, a channel for the work of the Holy Spirit in our lives. By encountering the promises of God, we are drawn into the life of God. As Peter wrote: "Thus

he has given us, through these things, his precious and very great promises, so that through them you may escape from the corruption that is in the world because of lust, and may become participants of the divine nature" (2 Peter 1:4). Put simply, God changes us as we read the Bible.

45. For Wesley, Scripture taught about salvation from beginning to end. In other words, Scripture teaches about the nature of salvation. Sometimes he called this the "whole tenor" or "general tenor" of Scripture. The "whole tenor of Scripture" expresses what Wesley would call "real religion," by which he meant God's work in restoring the divine Image in us that has been tarnished by sin, giving us "not barely deliverance from sin but being filled with the fullness of God" (John Wesley, "The End of Christ's Coming"). He also referred to it using a specific theological term, the "analogy of faith." Wesley writes: "Have a constant eye to the analogy of faith; the connexion and harmony there is between those grand, fundamental doctrines, Original Sin, Justification by Faith, the New Birth, Inward and Outward Holiness" (Preface, *Explanatory Notes Upon the Old Testament*). Put more simply, he reads all of Scripture through the lens of these four doctrines. He thought of this as the "plain sense" of Scripture. In other words, to understand the Bible, we should think of it as a book about salvation. Its subject is salvation, and its purpose is salvation.

46. Original sin refers to human beings' irresistible inclination to sin apart from Christ's work on the cross and the transforming power of the Holy Spirit. Sin is not just something we do, but a condition of the soul that distorts the Image of God in us. Justification by faith means that God forgives our sins if we put our whole trust in Christ for our salvation. The New Birth is a way of talking about God's work in our hearts that makes it possible for us to think, speak, and live in keeping with his will. In this way, the New Birth is a correction to Original Sin. Inward and outward holiness refers to the change that God works in our hearts throughout our lives, drawing us ever closer to him, restoring his Image in us, and bringing our will into agreement with his. The inward changes come through outward actions. We live differently because God has truly changed us inwardly. Joining Christians across the ages, John Wesley uses the terms *sanctification* and *holiness* to describe this.

The Old Testament Witness

47. Holiness is central to understanding the character of God in the Old Testament. An essential feature of holiness is that it refers to that which is set apart. God is unique and set apart from all that he has made. When the angels praise God, they cry out, "Holy, holy, holy is the Lord of hosts; the whole earth is full of his glory" (Isa. 6:3).

48. This major theme in the biblical story begins with the story of creation. After God created the whole cosmos, he created humanity in his Image. God is holy by nature, and since he created humanity in his Image, humans, too, share in God's holiness. Because of this, they reflect who God is. In other words, the invisible transcendent God will make himself known through the words and deeds of humans. God created us to be the visible representatives of his character and his purposes to the rest of the universe. Humans were to fill the earth and be stewards of it on behalf of the true King (Gen. 1:26–31). Care and witness were the key roles served by humanity. God's nature is holy love, and so God's initial design was for harmonious relationships between God, humans, and all of creation.

49. Humanity's holiness was marred when humans rebelled against God and human beings became separated from God. The rest of Scripture tells the story of how God made a way for humans to be restored through God's holy, unconditional love that transforms human relationships with God, self, and others. In the Pentateuch, the first five books of the Bible, we see God choosing to work through one particular family: Abraham and his descendants. After the people of God end up in Egypt and are subjected to slavery, God delivers them, leading them to Sinai. There he makes a covenant with them, saying, "You have seen what I did to the Egyptians, and how I bore you on eagles' wings and brought you to myself. Now therefore, if you obey my voice and keep my covenant, you shall be my treasured possession out of all the peoples. Indeed, the whole earth is mine, but you shall be for me a priestly kingdom and a holy nation. These are the words that you shall speak to the Israelites" (Ex. 19:4–6). In this covenant, the people of Israel are identified

as a *holy* nation—they have been set apart, distinct from the other nations around them, to worship and serve the Lord alone. And one of their purposes is to be a priestly nation, a group of people who demonstrate what it means to live as a holy people before the one true God. It is in this context that God gives the commands found in the Pentateuch.

50. The laws in the Old Testament teach God's people what it looks like to be a holy people set apart to the Lord. The broadest frame for this goal is twofold: love God with all one's being (Deut. 6:4–5) and love one's neighbor as one's self (Lev. 19:18b). The Ten Commandments (Ex. 20 and Deut. 5) illustrate loving God and loving neighbor. The opening commandments instruct Israel on the love of God, the Sabbath commandment bridges from the opening focus on love of God to the closing focus on love of neighbor. The framework of loving God and loving neighbor frames the rest of the Old Testament. The law codes give specific examples of what a life of holiness looked like in ancient Israel (Ex. 21–23; Lev. 17–26; Deut. 6–26).

51. The first command that God gives them is that they "shall have no other gods before me" (Ex. 20:3). Being a people who are set apart means having a focus on God as the one true holy God who makes covenant with his people. After the instructions of Exodus 20–24, God instructs the people of Israel to build a tabernacle. This will be a place where God's holiness can be present with his people without destroying them. God will dwell with his people at the very center of their camp—this can be seen as a partial restoration of Eden, where God walked in the garden with Adam and Eve. Yet, at the same time, only certain people will be able to approach the most holy place in the tabernacle where the presence of God resides. Only the high priest will be able to go there once a year to offer a blood sacrifice that provides atonement for the sin of the people. Through this sacrifice, Israel remains in right relationship with the holy covenant God. The other sacrifices required in the law form a similar function of enabling the people to maintain a holy relationship honoring God.

52. God continues to instruct his people, both through the sacrificial system and more broadly through lifestyle practices such as the Nazirite vow

in Numbers 6, calling them to be holy just as he is holy (Lev. 19:1–2). The instruction to be holy as God is holy will be repeated in the New Testament (Matt. 5:48; 1 Peter 1:16). This holiness is summed up in the instruction to love one's neighbor (Lev. 19:18). Such love means that the community cares for the poor (Lev. 19:10), deals truthfully with one another (Lev. 19:11–12), respects each other's property (Lev. 19:13), cares for the foreigner in their midst (Lev. 19:33–34), doesn't show preferences for people based on their economic status (Lev. 19:15), and doesn't mock those who are disabled (Lev. 19:14). In other words, being holy as God is holy involves care by the whole community for the whole community.

53. God promised that there will come a time when this call to holy living will be fulfilled. Through David, God said in Psalm 130:7–8, "O Israel, hope in the Lord! For with the Lord there is steadfast love, and with him is great power to redeem. It is he who will redeem Israel from all its iniquities." As a song that Israelites would sing as they approached the temple for worship (one of the Psalms of Ascent), this promise would be foremost in their minds and hearts as they prepare themselves to enter before the presence of the Lord. This helps create that longing for holiness of heart and life that John Wesley and Methodists proclaimed centuries later, specifically when Wesley quoted this passage as the scriptural proof of a "clear promise of this—that God will save us from all sin" (*A Plain Account of Christian Perfection*).

54. The purpose for Israel's call to be a holy nation was to serve as a light to the Gentiles, so that God's salvation may reach to the whole of the earth (Isa. 42:6; 49:6). The God of the cosmos cares for all of his creation—God's love for his special people, Israel, is only the beginning. Their purpose is to spread the holy love of God to all peoples. The problem in the Old Testament is that God's people fail to live out the love of God and neighbor. The two great sins of the Old Testament are idolatry and injustice. We practice idolatry whenever we attempt to hold multiple allegiances apart from a solitary commitment to the Lord. This was Israel's problem. They mixed their commitments to God with beliefs and commitments to other deities. The opposite of loving neighbor involves the failure of doing right for others and the failure to

extend mercy to those in need. God's people failed to live out the love of God and neighbor. Either they were guilty of worshipping false gods (not loving God with their whole hearts), or they were guilty of mistreating people like widows, orphans, and strangers (not loving their neighbors as themselves). In response, God sent the prophets, from Samuel to Malachi, and the Holy Spirit inspired these prophets to call Israel to repent (e.g., Isa. 1:16–17; Jer. 35:15; Joel 2:12–13), that is, to return to *faithfulness* in living out the love of God and neighbor (e.g., Amos 5:24; Micah 6:8; Mal. 3:7).

55. Ultimately, it is an issue of the heart. Both inner thoughts and outward actions matter to God. In Deuteronomy 30:6, Moses tells the people, "Moreover, the Lord your God will circumcise your heart and the heart of your descendants, so that you will love the Lord your God with all your heart and with all your soul, in order that you may live." Another passage addressing God's desire for a holy heart is Jeremiah 31:31–34, a passage alluded to by Jesus at the Last Supper, which states:

> The days are surely coming, says the Lord, when I will make a new covenant with the house of Israel and the house of Judah. It will not be like the covenant that I made with their ancestors when I took them by the hand to bring them out of the land of Egypt—a covenant that they broke, though I was their husband, says the Lord. But this is the covenant that I will make with the house of Israel after those days, says the Lord: I will put my law within them, and I will write it on their hearts; and I will be their God, and they shall be my people. No longer shall they teach one another, or say to each other, "Know the Lord," for they shall all know me, from the least of them to the greatest, says the Lord; for I will forgive their iniquity, and remember their sin no more.

56. Here is the promise that the call to holy living will be possible. Again, in Ezekiel 36:24–27 God states through the prophet:

> I will take you from the nations, and gather you from all the countries, and bring you into your own land. I will sprinkle clean water upon you,

> and you shall be clean from all your uncleannesses, and from all your idols I will cleanse you. A new heart I will give you, and a new spirit I will put within you; and I will remove from your body the heart of stone and give you a heart of flesh. I will put my spirit within you, and make you follow my statutes and be careful to observe my ordinances.

57. Lest we think that holiness is merely a list of rules, Isaiah reminds us that holiness is about living in peaceful relationship with God, and it results in joy and gladness:

> A highway shall be there,
> and it shall be called the Holy Way;
> the unclean shall not travel on it,
> but it shall be for God's people;
> no traveler, not even fools, shall go astray.
> No lion shall be there,
> nor shall any ravenous beast come up on it;
> they shall not be found there,
> but the redeemed shall walk there.
> And the ransomed of the LORD shall return
> and come to Zion with singing;
> everlasting joy shall be upon their heads;
> they shall obtain joy and gladness,
> and sorrow and sighing shall flee away. (Isa. 35:8–10)

58. Because holiness is about a restoration of the heart in right relationships with God and neighbor, and because those right relationships then show themselves in the ways we act because of it, God will not leave people in an unholy state. The restoration will not be truly implemented until the coming of Jesus Christ and the outpouring of the Holy Spirit on the Church, but the promise is here. As John Wesley said in *A Plain Account of Christian Perfection*:

> The privileges of Christians are in nowise to be measured by what the Old Testament records concerning those who were under the Jewish

dispensation; seeing the fulness of time is now come, the Holy Ghost is now given, the great salvation of God is now brought to men by the revelation of Jesus Christ. The kingdom of heaven is now set up on earth, concerning which the Spirit of God declared of old time, (so far is David from being the pattern or standard of Christian perfection,) "He that is feeble among them, at that day, shall be as David, and the house of David shall be as the angel of the Lord before them" (Zech. 12:8).

The New Testament Witness

59. Jesus Christ is the revelation of God who embodies holiness, the holiness of God in human form. The angel revealed to Mary that Jesus would be born holy (Luke 1:35) and would inaugurate the kingdom of God on earth. Jesus's life and teachings are the illustration of and invitation to the sanctified life. Jesus commands his disciples to repent and "follow me," inviting them into the life of communal and missional holiness (Matt. 4:19; 8:22). Jesus's disciples are called to hear and obey his teachings/commands (Luke 11:28; John 14:15). The Sermon on the Mount (Matt. 5–7) provides a concentration of Jesus's teaching about radical obedience to God's will, leading to a blessed life.

60. The pinnacle of our Lord's teaching is in the two Great Commandments—loving God wholeheartedly and loving one's neighbor as oneself (Matt. 22:37; Mark 12:30; Luke 10:27)—and in his "new commandment" to love one another after the pattern of Jesus's own self-giving love (John 13:14–15; see 15:13). Jesus's teachings were accompanied by the performance of miracles which demonstrate the powerful inbreaking of God's kingdom, bringing wholeness in body and spirit to human beings and defeating evil powers.

61. At the Last Supper Jesus revealed to his disciples that his blood is the cup of the new covenant (Luke 22:20) and his death will initiate the new covenant. On the cross, Jesus carried out the will of the Father, giving his disciples a pattern for the holy life that involves self-sacrifice. Jesus shows the self-giving love of God, offered to us even at the cost of his Son. Jesus's death paid the

price for human sin and his resurrection defeated sin and death, making it possible for those who follow him to live holy lives. Before Jesus's return to heaven, he commanded his disciples to be his witnesses and he promised to send his Holy Spirit who will remain with them until his return.

62. In Acts, Jesus tells his disciples to wait for the promise from the Father, the sending of the Spirit. Peter says that the promise of the Holy Spirit comes as a gift to those who repent of their sins (Acts 2:38). At Pentecost, the outpouring of the Spirit is the beginning of the fulfillment of God's promise to pour out his Spirit on people from every tribe, tongue, and nation. It is also at Pentecost that the gospel is proclaimed in a way that all can understand in their own language, showing that all people can live holy lives. The indwelling of the Spirit empowers the Church to proclaim boldly the forgiveness of sins and is a sign of God's sanctifying work in the lives of disciples, "cleansing their hearts by faith" (Acts 15:9). In Acts, the Holy Spirit brings about holiness in the Church—convicting of sin, directing, guiding, protecting, convincing, and empowering. God's people now have God's presence and power always with them to boldly live holy lives and testify to God's holy kingdom (Acts 28:23, 31).

63. The New Testament letters are directed to Christians to instruct them in holy living and to outline for us how to live into the realities of the kingdom of God. Key contributions related to holiness include teachings about who Christ is and the work that he has done (Rom. 3:21–26), living in community with God and one another, and the characteristics of those marked by the holy life. When Paul wrote about the gospel, he pointed to Abraham, whose life of faith foreshadows God's purpose of bringing people from all nations into right relationship with him through faith. Paul also saw Christ as the last Adam, whose atoning death reverses the curse of the first Adam's sin, which had corrupted humanity (Rom. 5:12–21). God's work in Christ creates a new humanity that is destined to be fully conformed to the Image of his Son (Rom. 8:29), who is himself the Image of the invisible God (Col. 1:15). God's new people are the body of Christ, which Paul sees as being united in faith and growing to maturity (perfection), that is, growing up "in every way into

him who is the head, into Christ" (Eph. 4:15). The Church's ministry aims to present every person "mature" (or "perfect") in Christ (Col. 1:28). Christian perfection represents a maturity in faith that can also be called perfect love.

64. Paul's teaching about holiness includes the beginning of salvation through justification by faith, which means pardon for sin based upon the reconciling work of Christ's death. Justified believers, those who have received forgiveness for their sins, are united with Christ in his death and risen life and therefore are "in Christ." However, for Paul, the fullness of salvation involves Christ truly dwelling in the hearts of believers (Eph. 3:17), or Christ "formed" in them (Gal. 4:19). The holy life begins by union with Christ in his death, which provides deliverance from the dominion of sin and death (Rom. 6:1–10); it includes considering ourselves "dead to sin and alive to God" (Rom. 6:11; see also vv. 12–14). This, however, may only be accomplished through the indwelling Holy Spirit who empowers believers to put to death the unrighteous deeds of our natural, fallen selves ("the flesh") and to live righteously (Rom. 8).

65. Paul expresses the holy life in numerous ways. One especially close to John Wesley's heart was Paul's command to have the same mind or attitude that was in Christ Jesus (Phil. 2:5). Knowing God's will may only happen through a transformation of the mind, as opposed to being conformed to the world (Rom. 12:2). In this context, Paul encourages believers to put off the patterns of their old self and to put on those of the new self, which has been renewed according to the Image of God (Col. 3:9–10; Eph. 4:22–24). The chief virtues that should be cultivated in the life of believers are faith, hope, and love—especially love, "which is the bond of perfection" (Col. 3:14 [lit. rendering]; see Eph. 4:22–24). Moreover, Paul exhorts believers to "walk in the Spirit" and, consequently, produce the fruit of the Spirit: love, joy, peace, patience, kindness, generosity, faithfulness, gentleness, and self-control (Gal. 5:22–23). The premier component of this fruit is "love," which fulfills the whole law (Rom. 13:9–10), which Wesley explicitly understood as a mandate for Christian believers to bear one another's burdens; visit the sick and imprisoned; and care for the poor, orphaned, and widowed. The effect is a life

dynamically related to God and others in consistent actions of praying continually, giving thanks in all things, and rejoicing evermore (1 Thess. 5:16–18).

66. In the other New Testament letters, the direct command to be holy is echoed from the Old Testament (Lev. 19:2). God's people are to "be holy, for I am holy" (1 Peter 1:16). As a result, we are formed as God's people into a "royal priesthood" and a "holy nation" (2:9–10). Just as in the Old Testament, we are now called to be visible representatives of God's holiness to those around us. Peter demonstrates this with an emphasis on good behavior in the presence of nonbelievers as an example of how to live in the world in a holy manner even when that involves suffering on account of one's faith in Christ Jesus. John Wesley emphasized the fact that holiness is more than just following a set of commandments from God; keeping God's commandments is rooted in a heart postured toward the love of God and the love of others, and is expressed in humility, faith, hope, and charity. James reminds us that life presents us with a choice between a life that is completely oriented toward God and a life that chooses our own desires and the way of evil. Holiness is both a way of life for the Christian today as well as part of God's promise for the future. As Christians, "we wait for new heavens and a new earth, where righteousness is at home" (2 Peter 3:13). In other words, as in Revelation, we look forward to a time when everything has been made right in the world and evil has been conquered and destroyed.

67. In the Old Testament, God's holiness was revealed through the commandments, the prophets, and the tabernacle where God dwelt with his people. Now God speaks to us through his Son (Heb. 1:2a), the one, true, only, and perfect sacrifice who atones for sin fully and completely. As it is written in Hebrews: "But when Christ had offered for all time a single sacrifice for sins, 'he sat down at the right hand of God,' and since then has been waiting 'until his enemies would be made a footstool for his feet.' For by a single offering he has perfected for all time those who are sanctified" (10:12–14). This perfect sacrifice cleanses the believer internally. This is in contrast to the Old Testament sacrifices which are described as incomplete—only able to cleanse the external person. Scripture testifies to this in the New Testament in

Acts 13:38–39: "Let it be known to you therefore, my brothers, that through this man forgiveness of sins is proclaimed to you; by this Jesus everyone who believes is set free from all those sins from which you could not be freed by the law of Moses." We see the same idea in Hebrews 10:1, which teaches that the law "can never, by the same sacrifices that are continually offered year after year, make perfect those who approach." Jesus then makes a new covenant in his sacrifice that enables those who belong to him to live in right relationship with him, with each other, and with those around them.

68. In Revelation, the final book in the New Testament, John wrote about a vision he had of a throne room where, day and night, four living creatures sing to the one on the throne, "Holy, holy, holy, the Lord God the Almighty, who was and is and is to come" (4:8). Later he sees a vision where only one is found worthy and able to open a scroll and its seals. Jesus, as the holy and bloodied Lamb of God, is that one. He is found worthy because he gave himself as a bloody sacrifice to allow people from every tribe, language, people, and nation to live in relationship with God and reign on earth (Rev. 5:9).

69. Those who follow Jesus are called to be faithful witnesses to Jesus Christ in suffering as he did, even to the point of death. By not resisting suffering and taking up our crosses now, we demonstrate the way of Jesus for all to see, looking to be vindicated in the age to come. As a result, the vision that John saw inspires hope for those who are experiencing persecution or suffering, knowing that it will not last forever. The vision found in Revelation culminates in the New Jerusalem, where God perfectly redeems and restores all of heaven and earth. This new creation excludes all things unclean (Rev. 21:27). The holy city and the tree of life are offered as shares for the saints in the age to come (22:19). God makes his home in this holy city that comes down from heaven: "He will dwell with them; they will be his peoples, and God himself will be with them; he will wipe every tear from their eyes. Death will be no more; mourning and crying and pain will be no more, for the first things have passed away" (21:3–4). God and his people dwell in pure holiness in being and doing.

70. Salvation now, by faith in Christ, prepares us for the new creation. John Wesley reminds us that salvation is both "instantaneous and gradual." A life fully immersed in the love of God results in the ever-increasing love of God and love of neighbor characterized by sharing in the mind of Jesus Christ and the fruit of the Holy Spirit. The Scripture commands us to be "doers of the word, and not merely hearers who deceive themselves" (James 1:22), and promises to transform us into a holy people as we encounter God and participate in his kingdom through the means of grace (meditating on Scripture, participating in prayer, and receiving the Lord's Supper, etc.). In the beginning, God created us to share in community with him and with one another. Original sin poses a conflict in our ability to love God and others. When God established a covenant with Abraham and his descendants, the story of redemption began and climaxes in the life, death, and resurrection of Jesus. When we receive the forgiveness of sin and accept his invitation to new life, the power of sin is broken and, by his Spirit, we are emboldened and empowered to live a good life. This is the good news at the heart of Scripture.

CHAPTER 3

The Triumph of Grace

The Universal Call to Holiness

71. At the center of a Wesleyan vision of holiness of heart and life we find holy love. But what is holy love? How do we describe it? It's not simply the love that we may have as humans for one another, as wonderful as that can be. Holy love is defined by God and who he is. Because "God is love" (1 John 4:8) and because God is holy (Isa. 6:3), holy love represents God's "absolute perfection" (*TFOD*, ¶23). This holy love, God's love, is expressed fully in Jesus Christ so that whoever believes in him is united with God in fellowship and has eternal life (John 3:16). We could say that the best way to define holy love is to look at Jesus; he's the ultimate example. And he invites us to walk with him.

72. All of creation was forged by God "in and for love" (*TFOD*, ¶63), and humanity was uniquely formed in God's Image. This Image in each person is an image of holy love and represents the relationship between God and humanity. This relationship of love was, and remains, God's intention for the whole world. However, because of sin, the Image of God's holy love has been marred and we all suffer from its effects (*TFOD*, ¶77).

73. Since God is holy and we are not, holiness on its own can seem to be God holding us at arm's length—God reminding us of all the ways that we are not like him, and our own awareness of our unworthiness (Isa. 6:5; Luke 3:16). But the holiness of God is not a distancing characteristic, something that pushes us away. It's a "drawing" characteristic, something that brings us near. Holy love is extended to all, not just to those who are deserving of it—because none are deserving of this love. The expression of this love is not dependent upon anything the object of that love can offer in return. Nothing we can do can justify it. God's holy love is constant, relentless, inviting, but never coercive.

74. In describing humanity, John Wesley wrote that the purpose of a person's life was "having 'fellowship with the Father and Son;' . . . joined to the Lord in one Spirit" ("The Circumcision of the Heart"). This purpose is not only for the Christian or for those already in the Church. Instead, this "fellowship" is for everyone. God's call to holiness is for the whole world. When humanity sinned and brought corruption to the created order, God immediately began the work of healing and the restoration of the divine Image. He sought out Adam and Eve in the garden (Gen. 3:9), saved Noah and his family from the flood (Gen. 7:7); and established a covenant with Abraham, Isaac, and Jacob, calling the people of Israel to be his own for the sake of this renewing work. But Israel's was not a calling for Israel alone. The covenant that God gave Israel was intended to bless the whole world. So when Christ fulfilled the covenant himself, that blessing now flows to every part of the creation and everyone in it.

75. In Christ, the covenant is not only completed—the agreement of God and humanity made perfect—but its universal nature is made plain in Christ's life, ministry, death, and resurrection. We can see in his life how he reached out to all those he encountered, regardless of race, sex, or status. And we can see in the effect of his work that his mission had cosmic effect not limited by time or space. His entire life is a testimony of God's will to be in relationship with us, and with us all, including his self-offering for all and his resurrection that began the new creation, a new creation intended for all. When Paul wrote to the Thessalonians that "this is the will of God, your sanctification" (1 Thess. 4:3), he was speaking not of God's will just for the faithful in that location but for all.

76. Christ's death on the cross was for the whole world. His death was not simply to justify us to God—to put us in right relationship with him—as wonderful a truth as that is, but his death also marks the point at which his ultimate self-offering makes possible the life of freedom (Rom. 8:2). The cross is not simply the end of Jesus's earthly ministry or a prelude to the resurrection, but a cosmic event where his death for us and for the

entire creation changed everything. His death is our reconciliation to God (2 Cor. 5:18–19). He died for all that all might be set free from the sin that separates us from God and from one another, to end the corruption of sin. He died to make us whole.

77. This wholeness means that holy love might reign in every heart, transforming our hearts so that they might mirror Christ's own. John and Charles Wesley's father, Samuel, wrote a hymn about this love:

> Behold the Savior of mankind
>   nailed to the shameful tree!
> How vast the love that Him inclined
>   to bleed and die for thee! ("Behold the Savior of Mankind")

78. Apart from the grace of God, we do not have the capacity to live lives of holy love, but through the grace of God we are set free from sin and empowered to love as God loves. We are enabled to have "the mind of Christ" (1 Cor. 2:16b). This work begins in us as individuals, but is always intended to be lived out with others as a community of faith. God set the pattern with Israel and now with the Church that he works with each of us, but ultimately wants to form a people who will then bless others. The people of God reflect this holy love to the world so that God's love may be seen in tangible ways. As we are patient and kind our relationships are transformed, "not envious or boastful or arrogant or rude." We do not insist on our own way; we are not irritable or resentful; we do not rejoice in wrongdoing but rejoice in the truth. We bear all things, believe all things, hope all things and endure all things (1 Cor. 13:4–7). Reflecting the nature of God, our Christian communities demonstrate this constant, faithful love of God to all. We are distinctly different from any other communities by being a living example of the possibility of the triumph of grace in all of our lives and relationships. We are not remarkable because we are a small gathering of super Christians, but because we are ordinary, everyday Christians who demonstrate the radical power of Christ to empower us with holy love.

New Birth

79. One of the central claims of the Evangelical Revival, of which early Methodists were a part, is that we can experience something called the new birth. If you heard one of the preachers of the revival, in churches or fields, it's very likely that you heard a sermon about the new birth. And they preached about it with passion! Jesus spoke of this new birth in John 3, when he taught the religious leader Nicodemus about the new life "from above" (v. 3). In John's account, we can see that this concept confuses Nicodemus because he asks:

> "How can anyone be born after having grown old? Can one enter a second time into the mother's womb and be born?" Jesus answered, "Very truly, I tell you, no one can enter the kingdom of God without being born of water and the Spirit. What is born of the flesh is flesh, and what is born of the Spirit is spirit. Do not be astonished that I said to you, 'You must be born from above.'" (vv. 4b–7)

80. The new birth is the moment we are brought by God from darkness to light, from sickness to health, and from sin to salvation. If justification breaks the guilt of sin, the new birth breaks its power. Scripture teaches us that being born again by the power of Jesus Christ makes us new: "So if anyone is in Christ, there is a new creation: everything old has passed away; see, everything has become new!" (2 Cor. 5:17). The new birth is a gift from God the Father, through the justifying work of the Son, born in our hearts by the Spirit through whom we are regenerated, which means we are empowered, made alive, to live in obedience to God and experience holy love.

81. Sin and its corrupting impact in us make the new birth necessary. Humanity was originally created in the Image of God, but because of sin that Image has been entirely corrupted. Yet when we are born again, the restoration of the Image of God is begun and, by God's work in us, we overcome both the guilt and power of sin. As the Scripture tells us: "You were taught to put away your former way of life, your old self, corrupt and deluded by its lusts, and to be renewed in the spirit of your minds, and to clothe yourselves with

the new self, created according to the likeness of God in true righteousness and holiness" (Eph. 4:22–24).

82. Justification and the new birth occur together in the soul of the new believer, although there is a difference in what they accomplish. Justification is "that great work which God does *for us*, in forgiving our sins," whereas the new birth is "the great work which God does *in us*, in renewing our fallen nature" (John Wesley, "The New Birth," italics original). The former implies a change relative to our status with God; the latter implies a real change in both heart and life (*TFOD*, ¶125). Through this real change we are empowered by the Spirit to grow in holiness through sanctification; we do not remain imprisoned to the sin that formerly separated us from God.

83. Receiving the new birth gives us an assurance of our salvation. The Holy Spirit gives us a spirit of adoption so that we come to know ourselves as children of God (Gal. 4:4–7). This isn't simply head knowledge though. This assurance is a deep-seated and experienced awareness of having been adopted as God's own. As Wesley writes: "even the testimony of their own spirit with the Spirit which witnesses in their hearts, that they are the children of God" ("Circumcision of the Heart"). This deeply personal experience of the Spirit allows us to trust in God's love for us even though we may still struggle with sin in our initial steps in sanctification.

84. The new birth, being born from above, or regeneration, as it is sometimes called, is the inward act of grace that brings us into the covenant family of God. The Bible has a number of images for this new reality: the household of God, the household of faith, a chosen people, a royal priesthood, a holy nation (Eph. 2:19; Gal. 6:10; 1 Peter 2:9).

85. Because of the change that is affected in the heart through the new birth, there are certain fruits that will come to mark the life of the believer. Chief among these are faith, hope, and love. The attainment of these "theological virtues" are only possible by grace, and enable us to hold firm to the knowledge of God and the hope of glory as we move toward fulfillment of the two

Great Commandments: love for God and love for neighbor. The experience of these virtues is not mere habit; rather, one of the joys of the new birth is the change in our affections. Love comes to "sit on the throne" of the heart of the believer, organizing our affections into holy desires (John Wesley, "On Zeal").

86. We also receive an awakening of our spiritual senses that allow us to have a true sense "of God and the things of God" (John Wesley, "Of Faith"). As Jesus counseled Nicodemus, "Very truly, I tell you, no one can see the kingdom of God without being born from above" (John 3:3). Wesley understood this process to be a "two-fold operation of the Holy Spirit," which involves "having the eyes of our soul both *opened* and *enlightened*." We are enabled to see "the *spiritual world*, which is all round about us" as well as "the *eternal world*, piercing through the veil which hangs between time and eternity" ("The Scripture Way of Salvation," italics original). This quickening of our senses is indispensable to a right perception of the nature of God, of the world as it is, and of the world as he desires it to be so that we can both grow in holiness and participate with God in the work of restoring his creation.

87. After experiencing the new birth, the life of the believer is continually sustained by the Holy Trinity: "God having quickened him by his Spirit, he is alive to God through Jesus Christ." As the believer walks in holiness of heart and life, he experiences a "spiritual respiration" with Father, Son, and Holy Spirit. "God is continually breathing, as it were, upon his soul, and his soul is breathing unto God," John Wesley taught. "Grace is descending into his heart, and prayer and praise ascending to heaven." The relationship of new birth to ongoing sanctification becomes clear: "And by this intercourse between God and man, this fellowship with the Father and the Son, as by a kind of spiritual respiration, the life of God in the soul is sustained: and the child of God grows up, till he comes to 'the full measure of the stature of Christ'" (Wesley, "The New Birth").

88. The new birth marks the beginning of our journey of sanctification. It is the moment when we are "inwardly renewed by the power of God" (Wesley, "The Scripture Way of Salvation"). With the love of God poured into the new

believer's life, he or she takes the first step in holiness. Yet it is only the first step. As Wesley teaches, the new birth "is a part of sanctification, not the whole; it is the gate of it, the entrance into it. When we are born again, then our sanctification, our inward and outward holiness, begins" ("The New Birth"). Through the new birth, we are ushered into the life that God means for us to live. Sanctification then "gradually increases from that moment," and our salvation "puts forth large branches, and becomes a great tree," anticipating that moment to come when, "in another instant, the heart [will be] cleansed, from all sin, and filled with pure love to God and man" ("On Working Out Our Own Salvation").

Grace upon Grace

89. The call to a holy life is a universal call "again and again mentioned in the Scripture" (John Wesley, *A Plain Account of Christian Perfection*). It is an invitation to an ongoing life of Christian discipleship. We need to learn what it means to walk with Christ and become like him. After the new birth, this intentional life of discipleship—perhaps called the process of sanctification—begins. Another way to put this is to say that the process of sanctification is continued training in what it means to be free in Christ, to live into the freedom made possible by God's grace. This life is empowered by God's grace and includes our faith and response. We understand that the sanctified life carries within it commitments to "intention, totality, purity, perfect love, discipline, and growth" (Frank Bateman Sanger, "The Wesleyan Doctrine of Scriptural Holiness"). Wesley's understanding of growth in grace, or grace upon grace, means that sanctification is a call to actual transformation.

90. Holy living is dynamic. Growth is central to what it means to be holy. But its growth requires faithfulness to the commands of Scripture both in intention and faithful response. As such, it's something that we live, not just a concept. The need for growth in a holy life (the idea of grace upon grace or continually sanctifying faith) is, for Wesleyans, simply the "norm" for all who believe. It's God's design for all who come to saving faith. We can see this in James 1:25: "But those who look into the perfect law, the law of liberty,

and persevere, being not hearers who forget but doers who act—they will be blessed in their doing." John Wesley taught that growth is required for all believers to demonstrate the holy life in good works. He believed that without good works no one could "reasonably expect that he shall be sanctified in the full sense" ("The Scripture Way of Salvation"). Growth in sanctification, then, is a deepening of faith, a call to growth into Christian maturity "until all of us come to the unity of the faith and of the knowledge of the Son of God, to maturity, to the measure of the full stature of Christ" (Eph. 4:13).

91. The grace of the sanctified life is lived out dynamically as we cooperate with God's intention for our lives. As we "work out [our] own salvation with fear and trembling . . . enabling [us] both to will and to work for his good pleasure" (Phil. 2:12b–13), the grace of sanctification results in a real inner spiritual change. This inner transformation is the restoration of the divine Image, resulting in a new way of life. This restored life is shaped by community and is perfected in the love of God and neighbor.

92. Wesley taught that Methodism's chief contribution to reform the nation, and especially the Church, was the doctrine of holiness. It is our mission as heirs of the eighteenth-century revival to offer holiness to the broader Church today. The call, though, is to an ongoing perfecting work of our hearts and lives in love, and not to sinless perfection. Wesleyans are called to "spread scriptural holiness" throughout the world ("'Large' Minutes of 1763") and to fashion our efforts in Christian ministry to model that truth. According to Albert Outler, "What mattered most was that 'going on to perfection,'" living the Christian life marked by: love (of God and neighbor); trust in Christ and the sufficiency of his grace; and deep joy of the Holy Spirit (*Theology in the Wesleyan Spirit*).

93. As one grows in the life of holiness, a seriousness about the ways of God and a devotion to Christ emerges. So Wesleyans are earnest to pray as the Prayer Book states: "Cleanse the thoughts of our hearts by the inspiration of thy Holy Spirit that we may perfectly love thee and worthily magnify thy holy name" in all that we say and do. We testify to the power of sanctifying grace,

of lives freed from the power of sin. Grace calls us ever deeper; grace that redeems and sanctifies and makes us fit for heaven.

Entire Sanctification

94. God in Christ pardons us in justification and makes us alive in him in the new birth. And he continues that work of restoration in the sanctifying work of the Holy Spirit, which culminates in our entire sanctification. Entire sanctification is the full restoration of the Image of God in the life of the believer. This begins in the new birth when God destroys the power of sin in the life of the believer and grants freedom, both from the guilt of sin and from the fear of God's righteous anger. But the goal is entire sanctification. Borrowing an analogy from John Wesley, the believer moves from the porch of repentance, through the door of justification, and into the house of "religion itself," which is sanctification ("The Principles of a Methodist Farther Explained"). Though sin has lost its power in the new birth, its presence still persists. We can all admit that, even after becoming followers of Jesus, we all wrestle with sinful thoughts, perceptions, and motivations, and still succumb to selfish desires, insecurities, and pride. As Wesley states, sin "does not reign, but it does remain" ("Repentance of Believers").

95. The faithful follower of Christ must address the reality of this lingering sin. For just as the unbeliever is called by God to recognize their own sinfulness and repent, so, too, are believers called to recognize the sin that remains and to repent. This repentance is closely tied to faithful action through the power of the Holy Spirit (which is grace)—stopping harmful behaviors, doing what is good, and practicing the means of grace, such as prayer, meditating on the Scriptures, receiving the Lord's Supper, and spiritual conversation and worship with other believers. God has chosen to use these ordinary practices as a means by which to extend grace to those who love him, as we yield to his purpose and presence with us. This evangelical repentance, confessed and acted upon in faith, opens us up to the realization of God's promises for full deliverance from sin in this life. As we read in Scripture: "A new heart I will give you, and a new spirit I will put within you; and I will remove from

your body the heart of stone and give you a heart of flesh. I will put my spirit within you, and make you follow my statutes and be careful to observe my ordinances" (Ezek. 36:26–27). This act of yielding to the work of God is what Wesley referred to as sanctifying faith (Acts 26:18). This sanctifying faith is the only condition for entire sanctification.

96. It is only through the sanctifying work of God that the Image of God is fully restored in us, resulting in people who are being made holy once again, and who now love as God loves. This is also what we call Christian perfection. But this perfection should not be thought of as the word is commonly understood. It is not some form of super-human power or angelic qualities. It is not freedom from ignorance, temptation, poor judgment, or bodily limitations (*TFOD*, ¶130). Rather, this is what Wesley often referred to as "perfect love" (1 John 4:18), which he described as being filled with the love of God and neighbor. It is the holy love of God spread abroad in the heart. All of this is the work of the Holy Spirit, received by the believer through sanctifying faith.

97. As God works to sanctify us fully, our lives become marked by several distinctive characteristics, which are the outworking of God's Image restored in us by the Holy Spirit. We are made free to become who God made us to be. When we have been transformed by God's sanctifying work, we begin to exhibit holy love for God and neighbor. Love of God is expressed as a heart that continually seeks to abide in God's presence and seeks to please God in every thought, attitude, and action. Wesley described this love by pointing to Psalm 73:25–26: "Whom have I in heaven but you? And there is nothing on earth that I desire other than you. My flesh and my heart may fail, but God is the strength of my heart and my portion forever." On the other hand, love of neighbor manifests as the consistent presence of the fruit of the Spirit in our lives. We become more loving, more joyful, more at peace, more patient, more kind, more generous, more faithful, more gentle, and more self-controlled (Gal. 5:22–23). Because the heart is now ruled by holy love for God and neighbor, confirmed by the presence of the fruit of the Spirit, we also experience a full assurance of faith, whereby all fear and doubt is gone (1 John 4:18; Heb. 10:22).

98. Sanctification is not just a future hope. We can expect it in our present life. It should also be understood as both a process and a moment. In other words, God's sanctifying work continues in us throughout our lives, and yet there is a moment of recognition when the cleansing of sin from our lives through the Spirit is made clear. This might be thought of as a journey (sanctification) with waypoints along the way (entire sanctification) that leads to an ultimate destination (glorification). Regarding the progressive nature of sanctification, Wesley (quoting Romans 8:13) wrote: "We are enabled 'by the Spirit' to 'mortify the deeds of the body,' of our evil nature; and as we are more and more dead to sin, we are more and more alive to God" ("The Scripture Way of Salvation").

99. In one sense, we can understand the progressive nature of sanctification as continuing to "run the race" (Heb. 12:1). But we can also experience a specific moment in time and space (entire sanctification), where we realize we now walk in the light of the triune God and have been cleansed from all sin (1 John 1:7). This is the Spirit-filled life (Eph. 5:18). It is the Christlike life. As Wesley encourages us, "expect it by faith, expect it as you are, and expect it now!" ("The Scripture Way of Salvation").

100. We should not consider entire sanctification to mean that we are done. We never outgrow our need to be filled with the Spirit and the holy love of God and neighbor. As long as we live, we will continue to grow from grace to grace through the presence of the Holy Spirit. But as we continue to grow, we do so with the assurance of faith that we belong to God and he to us. As Wesley said, "He will not only sanctify you wholly, but will preserve you in that state until he comes to receive you unto himself" ("On Perfection").

Glorification

101. Glorification is the climax of God's saving grace to humankind. It is the fullness of God's promise of redemption and the resolution to all sin and suffering, to which holiness leads us. Upon death, the believer enters into an experience of rest in the presence of God, which is the intermediate

state, during which we wait for the coming resurrection of the body into the new creation (Rom. 8:25). Glorification marks the entrance of resurrected believers into the new creation (*TFOD,* ¶134). Resurrected and exalted with Christ, in glorification we at last find the full and proper end (*telos*) of God's intention for humanity since the very creation itself.

102. The bodily resurrection of Christ made it possible that we, too, might be glorified, made partakers of his divine nature (2 Peter 1:4; Athanasius, *On the Incarnation*). Having been raised bodily from the dead, Christ is "the first fruits of those who have died" (1 Cor. 15:20; *TFOD,* ¶196), meaning that all who belong to him will be raised with him at his second coming. The resurrection of Christ is the pattern of the believer's resurrection (*TFOD,* ¶199). The same Spirit who dwells in believers will raise us from the dead at Christ's return (Rom. 8:10–11).

103. The Bible uses many rich images to express glorification as the full and complete goal of the process of salvation. These images are necessary because they point to reality which we can only begin to grasp with our minds but cannot yet fully comprehend. It is at the point of glorification that we will fully conform to the Image of the Son of God (Rom. 8:29). Before that time, we are on a pilgrim journey to an everlasting homeland that we yearn for but have never seen (Heb. 11:10–16; cf. 1 Chron. 29:15; *TFOD,* ¶211).

104. Holiness in the present is a foretaste of the final transformation to come. The renewal of our character in holy love points to the full renewal of our bodily life at the general resurrection, when "the creation itself will be set free from its bondage to decay and will obtain the freedom of the glory of the children of God" (Rom. 8:21). The believer's freedom from the power of sin points forward to the coming liberty of all creation. For on that day, as John Wesley said, "there will be a deep, an intimate, an uninterrupted union with God; a constant communion with the Father and his Son Jesus Christ, through the Spirit; a continual enjoyment of the Three-One God, and of all the creatures in him!" ("The New Creation"). Likewise, at the marriage feast at the culmination of time we will hear the God of love declare, "Be holy, and

be happy; happy in this world, and happy in the world to come . . . Holiness becometh his house for ever!" ("The Wedding Garment").

105. The call to holiness is not merely a duty or demand, but an expression—precious and full of hope—of God's invitation to the promise of being made whole. Its expression is a guarantee of God's ultimate full completion of his saving work in us, and of the redemption of all creation. Even suffering is a light preparation for the weighty blessing and trust awaiting us (2 Cor. 4:17). Truly, "becoming God's friend [is] the only thing worthy of honor and desire . . . [it] is the perfection of life" (Gregory of Nyssa, *Life of Moses*). Social holiness, which is the transformed life forged in community, is therefore both the corporate expression of this work of God and a foretaste of our living together with all God's people, citizens of the New Jerusalem from every place and every age, in the full communion and stewardship of that "life that really is life" (1 Tim. 6:19).

CHAPTER 4

Holiness and the Church: Social Holiness

Means of Grace

106. The call to holiness was not given to us without the means to attain it. We can see this in Scripture where Paul blesses the Thessalonian church: "May the God of peace himself sanctify you entirely; and may your spirit and soul and body be kept sound and blameless at the coming of our Lord Jesus Christ," to which he then adds, "The one who calls you is faithful, and he will do this" (1 Thess. 5:23–34). But that leaves the question of how. How will God go about this transformation? And the answer to that is the means of grace.

107. The means of grace include those practices of the faith in which we encounter God. This is key to the whole enterprise. God's grace is dynamic and relational; his grace is an outgrowth of his very presence. We should never forget the transforming, relational power of God's grace. It is not simply a divine disposition, it's divine power made possible by his very life. And God has provided means for us to meet him. They are the means by which God regularly dispenses grace to us, holding our life together as the Church (Acts 2:42–47). John Wesley defined the means as "outward signs, words, or actions ordained of God, and appointed for this end [or purpose]—to be the *ordinary* channels whereby he might convey" his love and grace to humanity that we might grow in Christlikeness ("The Means of Grace"). The means, therefore, are the regular avenues through which we might encounter God and allow him to work on and in us that we might grow in love and holiness.

108. The means of grace are varied. And while there are standard means of grace, their number is unlimited. Wesley spoke about them in two general categories: works of piety and works of mercy. God encounters us in both acts

of piety and in the ways we show love to our neighbors, living out the Great Commandment (Luke 10:27).

109. The means of grace foster Christ-centered community. It is within this Christ-centered community that the means are practiced. And it is within this community that we can see the outworking of the fruit of the Spirit as we experience the Christian life together. By sharing in this fellowship, we encounter deep friendship and authentic compassion. This is *koinonia*—the lifeblood of the Church that is experienced when Christians commit to one another to encourage, exhort, and uphold one another. It is essential that Christians abide in Christ and with one another just as Jesus described in John 15:5 where he said that he is the vine and we are the branches. As the branches, we bear fruit as a result of our relationship with Christ and one another. The fruit of this relationship is seen in loving participation in one another's lives, "watching over one another in love," as early Methodists described it.

110. The means of grace remind us that the Christian faith is an embodied faith. We practice our faith through the means of grace, many of them tangible. And we do so together. The means of grace, as acts that channel and deliver the grace of God, enable us to reflect his goodness in tangible ways, both within the Church but also in the world as we live out our faith in our daily lives. This embodied faith, also known as "holiness of heart and life," is an ongoing expression of the human encounter with divine grace. It is made possible by God's work in and through the means of grace, producing holy living, and moving participants both individually and collectively toward Christlikeness. This is the essence of moving onto perfection. In all of this, prayer (one of the means of grace) is foundational to our lives as Christians. Wesley understood prayer "whether in secret or with the great congregation" as vital to the Christian life. He claimed that "all who desire the grace of God are to wait for it in the way of prayer" ("The Means of Grace").

111. It is worth noting that grace is not given to us by the means in and of themselves; they are channels. Grace is from God. Also, grace is not given

to us because of our performance of these spiritual disciplines. Wesley put it bluntly when he said that "all outward means whatever, if separate from the Spirit of God, cannot profit at all" ("The Means of Grace"). The very word *grace* implies that these are actions ordained by God, not by humans, because grace is the unmerited, pardoning, and empowering action of God. Grace is God's work. As such, the means offer a possibility through which we might meet and encounter God and receive his grace. The means ought to lead us to love God and love neighbor in a deeper or more expansive way—allowing us to mature in Christian character and grow in holiness.

112. Wesley described various means of grace common to the Christian life such as: "searching the Scriptures; (which implies reading, hearing, and meditating thereon;) and receiving the Lord's Supper, eating bread and drinking wine in remembrance of him. And these we believe to be ordained of God, as the ordinary channels of conveying his grace to the souls of men" ("The Means of Grace"). These means of grace will be explored below. While the term *means of grace* might be familiar to Methodists, it is not exclusively a Methodist term. In fact, the term comes from the larger tradition of the Church, particularly the Church of England in which Wesley was formed and ministered. Other terms that refer to a similar set of activities include *spiritual disciplines* and *practices of faith*.

113. Generally speaking, three categories are used to group or understand the means of grace. The first is usually called the ordinary means of grace—those things that are ordained by God and consistent with the practices of the Church community:

- Prayer
- Bible reading
- Eucharist (i.e., Holy Communion)

Baptism can be included in this list, but it is not a repeatable act. So while it communicates regenerative grace to both infants and those of "riper years," it is distinct from the other means of grace that are all repeatable.

114. The second group is often called the prudential means of grace, those activities that are wise and prudent because doing them regularly is participating in the activities of loving God and neighbor. These include:

- Service to the poor, sick, infirm, and those on the margins
- Testimony/witness
- Singing the faith
- Fasting and/or abstinence
- Being in silence and solitude before God
- Simplicity of life

115. The third grouping can be called extraordinary means of grace—these things that are not necessarily seen in the life of Jesus but seen in tradition, and experience shows us that God can still work through them. John Wesley thought that these means of grace might serve for a season. We might include among them some of the historic practices of Wesleyan revivalism: band meetings, holy conferencing, camp meetings, the mourner's bench, lay preaching, and altar calls, among others. Today we might consider the creation or viewing of art, whether film, drama, or other media, as an extraordinary means of grace as long as it opens us up to the ways in which God is working in our lives. Exercise can be seen as stewardship of God's gift of the body and so a means of grace. Even cooking and baking as service to one another can be included. Human endeavors that enrich our lives and point us to God's goodness can all be included when they reflect the sentiment behind Paul's words, "And whatever you do, in word or deed, do everything in the name of the Lord Jesus, giving thanks to God the Father through him" (Col. 3:17).

Worship

116. Christian worship is the central defining act of the gathered Church. It is our shared encounter with God, bearing witness by the Spirit through the Son "to the glory of God the Father" (Phil. 2:11). As such, worship is vital to our journey as Christians; it forms us in holy love. In fact, worship and holiness cannot be separated. In worship we see a pattern of revelation and

response—our response to God's self-revelation in his Word and then our participation in the story of God's work in the world. In worship we enter by the Spirit into "the ceaseless worship of the communion of all the saints, both in heaven and on earth" (*TFOD*, ¶157). As Charles Wesley taught us to sing:

> Angels and archangels join;
> We with them our voices raise,
> Echoing thy eternal praise. (*Hymns on the Lord's Supper*)

117. In worship we join in the eternal gathering of heaven that cry "Holy, holy, holy." In worship, we admit and confess our sins and receive both cleansing and calling (Isa. 6:1–9; Rev. 4:8). Worship is a fulfillment of our ultimate purpose to glorify Jesus Christ (1 Cor. 10:31), to whom every knee will bend and every tongue confess that he is Lord (Phil. 2:10–11).

118. Worship is a means of grace, a channel through which the people of God are "formed in Christlikeness, to be edified, and empowered by the Holy Spirit to live holy lives for the sake of the world, fulfilling God's kingdom purposes" (*TFOD*, ¶160). When we worship, "we encounter Christ as the one who both judges and gives grace to his Church that the Church might be whole in him" (*TFOD*, ¶144). John Wesley taught, "The end [of worship] is the honour of God, and the edification of the Church; and then God is honoured, when the Church is edified. The means conducing to that end, are to have the service so administered as may inform the mind, engage the affections, and increase devotion" (*Commentary on the Roman Catholic Catechism*). The edification of the Church includes acts that are both formational and catechetical. Participation in liturgy, hymnody, prayer, the Scripture read and proclaimed, and the sacraments, shape us and give us a grammar of faith. They also give us an identity as God's people, as through these means we are conformed to the Image of Christ the Son. We, therefore, commit ourselves to "not neglecting to meet together" (Heb. 10:25), but to gather in worship as we "bear witness to our identity as God's people as we celebrate the grand narrative of God's eternal activity" (*TFOD*, ¶160).

The Sacraments

119. The sacraments are central to the Church's worship and the journey of holiness. Baptism and Holy Communion are the two sacraments given by Christ to his Church (*TFOD,* ¶166), and he commands us to practice them (Matt. 28:19; 1 Cor. 11:23–25). Embedded in the grace-filled life of the Church, they are the particular means of grace by which the Church is made "a royal priesthood, a holy nation, God's own people" (1 Peter 2:9; cf. Ex. 19:6). As "outward signs"—something visible and tangible—they are the sacramental acts that set us apart to God and are public affirmations of our union with him. They make us and mark us as Christ's own and act as signs that our lives are now "hidden with Christ in God" (Col. 3:3). When we receive them in true faith and repentance, they become the ordinary channels of God's inward grace—the work that we cannot see, but can experience—given to us by the Holy Spirit. They both convey to us the holiness that is ours in Christ, and grant us the grace to grow to become like him, conformed to his Image (Rom. 8:29).

Baptism

120. Baptism (*TFOD,* ¶¶168–70, John Wesley "Treatise on Baptism") is the sacrament by which we are first set apart to God in Christ, the unique and definitive sacrament of our holiness in him. In baptism, we are no longer our own; we belong to God (1 Cor. 6:19). Baptism can only be performed once in a person's life. As the sign of our incorporation into Christ's body, baptism parallels the Old Testament's covenantal sign of circumcision. Yet the grace of baptism is a "spiritual circumcision" (Col. 2:11), a circumcision of the heart (Rom. 2:29; John Wesley, "Circumcision of the Heart"). Wesley taught that in the waters of baptism, the Holy Spirit works so that we die to ourselves and live to Christ; we are cleansed and made new. As such, baptism is also the means of grace by which we are united to Christ in his death and resurrection, being "buried with him in baptism" and "raised with him through faith in the power of God" (Col. 2:12). It is the sacrament by which we "were washed, . . . were sanctified, . . . were justified in the name of the Lord Jesus Christ and

by the Spirit of our God" (1 Cor. 6:11). As our Lord was anointed with the Holy Spirit at his baptism, so we, too, are baptized with the Holy Spirit in ours (Acts 2:38), made alive in him. Thus, those who are baptized are together "a temple of the Holy Spirit" (1 Cor. 6:19), a "new creation" (2 Cor. 5:17) "created in Christ Jesus for good works" (Eph. 2:10). Baptism is the sacramental means of our being made holy to God in Christ, and the beginning of our being conformed to his Image. As such, baptism is also the proper prerequisite for the sacrament of Communion.

121. That infants are included within the covenant promises of baptism is clearly affirmed by the witness of the Church since the time of the apostles, by the Wesley brothers (John Wesley, "Treatise on Baptism"), and by many Christians in the Wesleyan tradition. Baptism is, after all, the work of God. As children of believers, they are holy to the Lord (1 Cor. 7:14), members of the family of the Church (Acts 2:39), and recipients of the grace of baptism "through the water of rebirth and renewal by the Holy Spirit" (Titus 3:5). As they grow, they, too, must "grow in the grace and knowledge of our Lord and Savior Jesus Christ" (2 Peter 3:18) through faith and repentance, bearing the fruit of the Spirit as evidence of their salvation.

Eucharist

122. Wesley taught that Holy Communion is "the grand channel whereby the grace of his Spirit was conveyed to the souls of all the children of God" ("Upon Our Lord's Sermon on the Mount VI"). Instituted by Christ and given to the Church as a gift, it is a vehicle through which, by faith, we experience the sanctifying grace of God (Luke 22:19). When the Church gathers around the table of Christ, we remember the sacrifice that Christ made for our sins, encounter the very real presence of Christ, and proclaim his death until he comes again in final glory (1 Cor. 11:26). By participating in this holy meal, the Church experiences "the forgiveness of our past sins and the present strengthening and refreshing of our souls" (Wesley, "The Duty of Constant Communion"). In turn, we are sanctified by the Holy Spirit to turn away from sin in this life and freely embrace holy living ("The Duty of Constant Communion").

123. As the Church repeatedly receives the body and blood of Christ, she is increasingly united with Christ and given the transformational power of holy love. For this reason, John Wesley required Methodists to receive the sacrament of Holy Communion as often as possible, at minimum once a week. Nourished by grace, we are then emboldened to participate in the redeeming work of the Holy Spirit in the world.

124. Holy Communion is also a preview of the world to come, when Christ returns and the Church is fully united in perfect love with Christ. Charles Wesley wrote about this among the hymns that he penned to help the early Methodists understand the mystery of the Eucharist:

> O that we now thy flesh may eat,
> Its virtue really receive,
> Empower'd by this immortal meat
> The life of holiness to live:
> Partakers of thy sacrifice
> O may we all thy nature share,
> Till to the holiest place we rise,
> And keep the feast forever there. (*Hymns on the Lord's Supper*)

125. When Christ comes again, we will join with the angels and saints surrounding the throne, casting our crowns before Christ, the sacrificed and risen King, as we feast at the heavenly holy meal. Lost in wonder, love, and praise, we will see God's full restoration of the creation he loves. The perfect love and holiness of God—Father, Son, and Holy Spirit—will be shed abroad in the new heaven and new earth for all eternity (*TFOD*, ¶174).

Singing Holiness

126. When we gather to sing the praises of God, our congregational song speaks of God's holiness. Proclaiming and affirming the faith through song stirs our hearts and nurtures our affections toward a life of holy love. From the very beginning, singing has always been a defining feature of Christian

worship. God's people gather in worship to sing praises to God, to proclaim his holy character and work, and to testify of their gratitude for the experience of holy love. This stands in a long line of ancient worship, largely sung, from which souls have been nurtured in the faith.

127. Singing unifies the Church; we sing together both in heaven and on earth. When we gather together in worship in our local communities, we experience something not limited by time or space. In fact, the worship that we experience in the local setting "foreshadows our eternal vocation of praise" and "is also a participation, in real time, in the ceaseless worship of the communion of all the saints, both in heaven and on earth" (*TFOD*, ¶157). The act of singing is an example of the Church operating as the one, holy, catholic, and apostolic body of Christ. Charles Wesley wrote in one of his famous hymns "O for a Thousand Tongues to Sing":

> Glory to God, and praise and love
> be ever, ever giv'n
> by saints below and saints above,
> the church in earth and heav'n.

128. When we worship God in song, our singing becomes a means of grace. John Wesley differentiated between "instituted" means of grace (those that Christ instructed believers to do, such as the Lord's Supper, fasting, prayer, searching the Scriptures, and Christian fellowship) and "prudential" means of grace (other means that are beneficial for advancing spiritual growth). Singing in worship is a prudential means of grace. It is a helpful, prudent, God-honoring means for presenting ourselves before God to continue the ongoing process toward Christlikeness.

129. The greatest example of congregational singing in Scripture is the Psalms. The Psalms are sung and have often been called Israel's hymnbook. Congregational singing today mirrors the Psalms in its pattern of revelation and response. Singing is a direct engagement with God through proclamation, exhortation, testimony, praise, petition, and a call to works of piety and

mercy. It informs the Church about God and his holy love, work, character, and nature. It also invites the Church to participate in the life of Jesus Christ, reminding us of the story of his life, ministry, and ultimate triumph.

130. The Wesley brothers taught believers to sing the Christian faith. They emphasized singing because they believed the inner experience of salvation and the witness of the Holy Spirit would produce the outward praise of God. In other words, God's transforming work within us often inspires us to sing! The Wesleys also considered singing to be a powerful means for teaching the faith and orienting our love to its rightful end. For the Wesleys, congregational song bears witness to the truth, goodness, and beauty of God's saving grace through Jesus Christ—a grace that is powerful enough to convert any individual from a life of sin to a life of holy love. Charles Wesley wrote about this when he penned the words in the hymn "And Are We Yet Alive":

> Preserved by pow'r divine
> to full salvation here,
> again in Jesus' praise we join,
> and in His sight appear.

131. Charles Wesley's thousands of hymns provide in poetic form the work of God's grace. One of his gifts to the Church was his ability to use poetry to describe the wonder and mystery of God that is often beyond the grasp of mere words. It's not easy to describe God, salvation, or even holiness at times without stretching the capabilities of speech. Poetry helps us to do this, and Charles Wesley's poetry remains one of the best examples of this poetic theology. His hymns are filled with scriptural imagery, affectionate expression, and testimony to the work of God. We can see this in so many of his hymns and poetical works, but particularly in hymns such as "A Charge to Keep I Have," "Christ the Lord Is Risen Today," "Love Divine, All Loves Excelling," and "O for a Thousand Tongues to Sing," among others.

132. But the Wesley brothers cared for more than just the texts of the songs of worship. They cared even more for the humble heart singing them. Singing

can be a great gift, but it is not meant for self-gratification. We are not to use the gift of song to show off. As believers, our song should glorify God and edify the whole body of Christ (see John Wesley's "Ten Rules for Singing"). Only then will it be a means of grace to us and to those around us.

Preaching Holiness

133. For John Wesley, preaching is more than just speech. He saw it as beginning with the incarnation, the Father's sending of the Son. In preaching, the Spirit communicates the beauty of holy love to hearers in particular times, places, and circumstances (*TFOD*, ¶161). As Wesley states: "to the right person, to the right extent, at the right time, with the right aim, and in the right way. . . . the love of God and man not only filling my heart but shining through my whole conversation" ("An Address to the Clergy"). The gospel shapes both the speaker and the hearer.

134. Preachers are called to proclaim the good news of Jesus Christ, crucified and risen. His beauty resonates in us, producing love for God and the neighbors to whom we speak. Wesley spoke of God's "design" in raising up the preachers called "Methodists," which was "to reform the nation, and in particular the Church, to spread scriptural holiness over the land" ("'Large' Minutes of 1763"). There is an aesthetic dimension, even attractiveness, to the design of scriptural holiness as a form of life that embodies the simple beauty of loving devotion to God and service to neighbors according to the pattern of Jesus Christ.

135. Sharing the good news with others was for Wesley the fruit of a larger purpose. He saw it as an outgrowth of God's work in us to pardon and make us whole. In other words, we have been made new by God and the response is to share it. Sermons prayerfully communicated the message of Scripture, Christian tradition, and the lives of the saints. Preaching in early Methodism spoke to the extravagant love of the Father who, by sending the Son in the power of the Spirit, calls and creates a holy people in the world. Personal conversion, social change, and numerical growth, therefore, were not the

end or goal of preaching. Rather, these were celebrated as a witness to God's mercy as the Spirit called listeners to new life. The response was a sign of God's kingdom coming "on earth as it is in heaven" (Matt. 6:10) through the reign of Jesus Christ.

136. Preaching in the Wesleyan tradition is a calling to proclaim the gospel of God revealed and enacted in Jesus Christ. Bearing scriptural witness to the person and work of Christ, preachers summon God's people to align themselves with the Father's holy will. Preaching has the ability to remind us again of our purpose as human beings, illumined and empowered by the Spirit. For Wesleyans, the fullness of salvation is understood as the complete restoration of the deformed Image of God (*TFOD*, ¶162). This is the sanctification of the whole person—the intellect, affections, and will. This life is the new creation that is freely offered to all who receive it by faith. It comes by hearing the word of Christ through Scripture as discerned in the Spirit by faithful preachers.

137. The preaching of holiness calls Christian people to continue in the way of discipleship. Both its personal and social repercussions will require preachers who themselves are answering Christ's call to perfection. In this divine and human work, preachers will be devoted above all else to God, committed to maturing in the knowledge and love of God. This "holy preaching," or "preaching in the Spirit," becomes a living witness. Such preaching will be displayed in transformative power that bears fruit in the hearts and lives of God's people. And this is all of God, received humbly with glad and generous hearts.

138. Holy preaching, then, will be offered to God and his people as an act of worship, the surrender of the preacher's speech and life to the living God. There is great freedom in the preaching of holiness—freedom from excessive and distracting focus on the preacher or people, as well as freedom for contemplating the Word in Scripture and responding in loving obedience.

139. The preaching of holiness, in both its personal and social expressions, will, in all times and places, sound rather odd and strange to many listeners.

This is because holiness, or God's "otherness," evokes and empowers Christian speech that reflects and shares in the otherness of Christ. Such "otherness" will be received as the Church's gift, witness, and mission to the world. Holy preaching will, therefore, be an act of obedient love for God and neighbor according to the pattern of Christ embodied in the way of self-giving love. Put simply, our preaching aims to make saints (*TFOD*, ¶165).

Watching Over One Another in Love

140. The process of sanctification "characterizes the life of serious Christian discipleship as believers grow in grace" (*TFOD*, ¶127). A core component of this process is rooted in relationships formed in and nurtured by the Church. For example, a young man returning to college found two other young men to share an apartment for their final semesters of college. Complete strangers to one another at the start, they quickly bonded as brothers in Christ. After a time, two of them began to notice that the third was deeply troubled by some unspoken problem. One evening, after finishing dinner, the two pulled their chairs close to the third, looked him directly in the eye, and said, "We're not getting up from here until you tell us what is bothering you." They demonstrated the "watching over one another in love" so characteristic of Wesleyan convictions about the process of sanctification within the fellowship of the Church.

141. Justification by faith, simultaneous with new birth, marks the beginning of the sanctified life as God's chosen children. The Church is an indispensable context for this ongoing work. Through the body of Christ, we learn to run the race and to walk in the narrow way that leads to life everlasting (Heb. 12:1–2; Matt. 7:13–14). In these days of easy virtual access to people, we stress that this work is by far best done face-to-face.

142. The goal of perfection, therefore, certainly has an individual dimension (one's heart must be fully engaged), but it is also deeply communal (the two cannot be separated). In Discourse 4 of John Wesley's series on the Sermon on the Mount, he reminds us: "Christianity is a social religion, and to turn

it into a solitary religion, is indeed to destroy it." As we grow in grace and the knowledge of God (2 Peter 3:18), we experience and pursue a core aspect of the work of salvation, which is to make us manifestations of divine love (Matt. 5:13–14).

143. We engage in working out our salvation (Phil. 2:12–13) through the means of grace in the Christian community. Class meetings help those who are beginning to "walk in the light" (1 John 1:7). They are the first experience of being loved and learning how to watch over one another in love. Band meetings move believers "on toward perfection" (Heb. 6:1) through the self-emptying of transparent confession (James 5:16), bringing the dark parts of our lives into the light. The traditional questions asked in the band societies therefore help group members "walk in the light as [God] himself is in the light" (1 John 1:7–9). The reality of being fully known and loved by one's small group directly reflects God's knowing and loving us fully.

144. The other means of grace are also communal. Reading the Bible is not only an individual exercise. People sharing their scriptural insights and questions help each other grow. Fasting, which contributes to our awareness of remaining sin, motivates us to confession and repentance. Praying together strengthens the bonds of love. Serving others, especially outside the Church, contributes to our growth in grace. Wesley reminded Methodists that visiting the sick is as much a means of grace for the visitor as it is for the visited ("On Visiting the Sick").

145. These practices interact through the Holy Spirit's grace work to transform the heart according to the vision of Ephesians 4. Believers committed to preserve the unity of the Spirit in the bond of peace and to "grow up in every way into him who is the head, into Christ" (v. 15) find themselves moving together, going on to perfection, from grace to grace, toward the full measure of the stature of Christ (v. 13).

CHAPTER 5

Holiness in Practice: The Church's Witness

Love for Neighbor

146. Any reflection on the place of holiness in Methodist and Wesleyan traditions is only complete after a deep consideration of "holy love" for our neighbors. From its very beginning, Methodists have practiced a Christianity that insists that holiness is rooted not only in personal and corporate piety, but also bears witness to the world that God's love is for all persons.

147. Perhaps the best example of God's desire for all to know him, and of our human tendency to only truly love those who love us, is the story of Jonah. In this story, God reached out to Jonah and told him to go preach to the Ninevites about the need to repent from their evil ways. Jonah, however, wanted nothing to do with this request for two reasons. First, he wanted nothing to do with them because he despised the Ninevites. And with good reason, for the Ninevites were bitter enemies of the Israelites. He did not want them to find out that God loved them. And because of this, Jonah, secondly, didn't want to preach because he knew God was gracious and would forgive them if they repented. The book ends with Jonah sulking under a tree because indeed, after he called the people to repent, God forgave them and demonstrated his love and compassion for all, even for some of the world's great sinners.

148. Methodist communities have demonstrated holy love for the world in many ways over the last three hundred years through social witness, compassion for all kinds of poverty, education, peacemaking, combating racism and gender inequality, and caring for the body, among other efforts. Often our efforts as Methodists have been incomplete, inadequate, and misguided. Nevertheless, we continue to strive for a perfect love for others in every aspect of our human existence.

149. Methodists have always insisted that any vision of holiness must include this love for neighbor. We look to the biblical vision of love as seen in Matthew 22:37–40, where the greatest commandments are to love God and then to love our neighbor as we love ourselves. We claim that God's love is indeed for all people, as seen most profoundly and concisely in John 3:16. First John 4:19–21 further emphasizes that loving God is intrinsically linked to loving one's neighbor, because God himself is love.

150. John Wesley makes it clear that compassionate and loving actions toward others are integral to Christian conceptions of holiness. In "The Scripture Way of Salvation," he claims that true faith involves a heart transformed by love, resulting in a life marked by loving deeds. In another work, *A Plain Account of Christian Perfection,* he describes Christian perfection as not the absence of faults but the presence of perfect love—a love that encompasses both God and neighbor.

151. Holiness is intrinsically linked to social witness because the basis and *telos* (goal) of our engagement with society find their source in God's call for his people to live in ways that represent him faithfully. It is a call that is relational at its core and lived out in and through communal interactions. It is an invitation from God for his people to embody a way of life that is in full alignment with his nature and will for humanity (Gen. 17:1–2; Lev. 19:2–3; Rev. 4:9–11; Ex. 20). This call is lived out in a trifold expression that is demonstrated through: (1) *being*—our individual and/or communal dispositions; (2) *doing*—the tangible acts that we perform and omissions we opt to make; and (3) *becoming*—the inner transformation that takes place in our lives as we continually draw closer to God and live in harmony with his children, our neighbors.

152. *Hospitality* is perhaps the best term that encapsulates a Wesleyan understanding of the love of the stranger. At its core, hospitality serves as the basis of our engagement with the world and a Christian invitation to a holy life. To be hospitable as Christians means to love all, especially the

poor, widows, and the stranger. God made clear to Israel the importance of caring for "the other," and throughout Scripture, the people of God are known for and by their hospitality (Deut. 10:19; 27:19; Lev. 19:34; cf. Matt. 5:43–44; Rom. 12:13; Heb. 11:31; 13:1–3; James 2:20, 25–26). Hospitality is the core of our social witness because the invitation to be in covenant with God and to enter into a relationship with him is for the sake of others (Gen. 12:1–3; 1 Peter 2:9–10).

153. When the holy love of God fills a person's heart, it leads to a life of obedience and submission, from which flows genuine and holy love for others. This love finds expression in acts that are honorable and pleasing to God and in lasting and healthy relationships that include and necessitate tangible acts of mercy. In this way, holy love for others is the foundation of all Christian hospitality. Hospitality is the essence of holy love for our neighbor, and the bedrock for the Church's witness to an unbelieving world. Holiness and Christian witness are intertwined because the *telos* of our love-filled and hospitable engagement with the world is both transforming and transformative. A rightly ordered life of holiness bears witness to the love of God and the beauty of the Christian community.

154. The Israelites were often reminded that their way of life was a conduit to raise awareness and curiosity about God (e.g., Deut. 6:20). Living a life of holy love is an invitation to the essence of human flourishing as understood in divine revelation. Such flourishing, it is important to note, is not a life free of suffering. The word *witness* (*martureo*) includes the possibility of suffering and sacrifice in its meaning. While Wesleyans do not idealize suffering and sacrifice, we understand that throughout Scripture and the history of the Church, people who have endeavored to live faithfully in light of the Christian story have experienced various kinds of suffering. Indeed, our greatest example of a life of love and holiness is found in our Savior, Jesus Christ. Our social witness is itself a form of discipleship that takes on the cruciform nature of the life of our Lord and Savior.

Holiness and Poverty

155. Wesleyans believe that a robust vision of holiness will address more than material poverty, but all aspects of human impoverishment. We consider the definition of poverty to be: the absence of substance that produces liberty for spiritual, material, and relational flourishing. In *The Character of a Methodist,* John Wesley equates love of neighbor and care for the poor with qualities of being a Methodist. He even goes so far as to suggest that works of mercy are a means of grace by which a person grows in sanctification. He regularly advised affluent people to visit the poor in order to "improve life" and "use their health."

156. Wesley's model for addressing the needs of the poor came from Scripture: "Blessed are you who are poor, for yours is the kingdom of God" (Luke 6:20); "The Spirit of the Lord is upon me, because he has anointed me to bring good news to the poor" (4:18); "I was hungry and you gave me food, I was thirsty and you gave me something to drink, I was a stranger and you welcomed me, I was naked and you gave me clothing, I was sick and you took care of me, I was in prison and you visited me" (Matt. 25:35–36); and "Jesus, looking at him, loved him and said, 'You lack one thing; go, sell what you own, and give the money to the poor, and you will have treasure in heaven; then come, follow me'" (Mark 10:21). When Jesus offered spiritual food to the crowds, he recognized the people's physical hunger and paused to meet their material need. Beautifully, he incorporated a young boy's lunch into his miraculous provision (John 6). We, too, can experience Jesus's generous gift of substance to people in need as we offer our resources to him.

157. The Epistle of James explicitly joins faith and works as he commends true worship: "Religion that is pure and undefiled before God, the Father, is this: to care for orphans and widows in their distress, and to keep oneself unstained by the world" (1:27). James's example speaks to a nearly universal situation of poverty, that of fatherless families "in distress." But this meeting of human needs does not stand alone as the pure and undefiled religion that pleases God; it is paired with one aspect of holiness, "keep[ing] oneself unstained by

the world." James goes on to challenge believers in their practice of favoring the rich:

> My brothers and sisters, do you with your acts of favoritism really believe in our glorious Lord Jesus Christ? For if a person with gold rings and in fine clothes comes into your assembly, and if a poor person in dirty clothes also comes in, and if you take notice of the one wearing the fine clothes and say, "Have a seat here, please," while to the one who is poor you say, "Stand there," or, "Sit at my feet," have you not made distinctions among yourselves, and become judges with evil thoughts? Listen, my beloved brothers and sisters. Has not God chosen the poor in the world to be rich in faith and to be heirs of the kingdom that he has promised to those who love him? (2:1–5)

158. Christians are called to similarly give of themselves. If each of us is created in the Image of this triune God, and poverty of all kinds (material, social, and spiritual) exists, then Christians respond with "acts of mercy," seeking to help people to be restored to the Image of God. God's best for people, the holy life, would be that they never experience poverty. Holy people engage the world with hospitality (*xenophilios*; Rom. 12:13) to help people realize all they were created to be.

159. Those who experience poverty should not be seen as objects of our charity, but as people created in the Image of God with capacity to move toward true fulfillment in Christ. All of humanity experiences poverty of some kind, and we together respond to God's work in the world, to help each other to move beyond the absence of the "restored image" that we all experience at some level. This approach creates an attitude that moves beyond objectifying others with a paternalism that can be toxic to all involved.

160. Nevertheless, our shared creation in the Image of God means that Christians are called to be with those who experience poverty. John Wesley noted in his sermon "On Visiting the Sick" that "One great reason why the rich, in general, have so little sympathy for the poor, is, because they so seldom

visit them." Christian holiness entails seeking opportunities to demonstrate acts of mercy as often as possible to help others experience God's best for their lives—holiness. Each kind of poverty requires a different response. Material poverty of an emergency nature (e.g., natural disasters) requires immediate material response. Other varieties of material poverty (e.g., homelessness, addictions) require more developmental and rehabilitative responses that move beyond temporary solutions.

Education

161. A Wesleyan understanding of education is rooted in a vision of holy love, particularly one that engages the poor. Beginning with the Kingswood School in 1748, Methodist hopes for education have historically been focused, first and foremost, on revealing the person of Jesus Christ. By centering its work around Christ, the educational experience at these institutions trains students in habits of heart and mind that prepare them to partner with God's work in the world. Wesleyan movements have often promoted education for the common good, be it in the formation of boarding schools for the children of itinerant preachers, literacy centers for the impoverished, or primary schools and higher education institutions throughout the world. Education brings the individual closer into the fullness of human flourishing. Offering such an education to the public is a form of Wesleyan social witness.

162. In the nineteenth century, Wesleyans established primary schools and colleges to propagate holiness doctrine through the education of young people. John Wesley Hughes was the founding president of Kentucky Holiness School, which would eventually become Asbury University. He stated the purpose of the new college in a way that also reflects the purpose for many Methodist schools as "a distinctly religious school where young men and young women can get a thorough College education under the direction of a faculty composed of men and women wholly consecrated to God."

163. For Methodists, education was a way to love our neighbors by linking knowledge and piety, or as Charles Wesley stated, to "unite the pair so long

disjoin'd, knowledge and vital piety." Far from a reactive attempt to withdraw students from the world and insulate them from secular society, holiness-oriented education serves to promote growth in holiness among students along with a robust intellectual engagement with the world in which they live and serve. Wesleyan colleges help students develop patterns and dispositions of holy love and equip them to recognize how what they are learning in the classroom has relevance to the Church's social engagement with society. In this sense, a Wesleyan higher education serves as a social witness of the gospel through the living witness of graduates who serve Christ and impact the world in their communities and workplaces.

164. The integration of faith and learning is no small task. To be Christ-centered, Christian education must be biblically centered, and the Bible must hold primacy as a guide and key component of the curriculum. As John Wesley described himself as "*homo unius libri*" (man of one book), so, too, must Christian education center on biblical revelation, even as it exposes people to concepts and ideas that are not particularly Christian in nature. Seeking truth in any aspect of life and nature, Wesleyans believe, is critical to education. Education is an extension of and testament to social holiness, as the learning community also functions as a social ground for learning to love our neighbor in the midst of various backgrounds, experiences, and opinions. Educational institutions provide students of all ages the opportunity to come together in a focused environment for the purpose of this enrichment. The community is a place for testing, affirming, and teaching sound curriculum and doctrine.

165. Within the learning community, Christian education aims to foster humility and contemplation. As individuals become wiser, they recognize all the more the limits of human comprehension, a gap in which the Holy Spirit, through faith, flourishes and encourages. As John Wesley wrote: "[Faith] gives a more extensive knowledge of things invisible . . . for it does not leave us to receive our notices of them by mere reflection from the dull glass of sense; but resolves a thousand [mysteries] of the highest concern by giving faculties suited to things invisible" (Letter to Conyers Middleton).

166. Since their beginning, Wesleyan educational institutions have functioned to teach students to submit their vocations and callings to the broader work of the kingdom of God. For many educational institutions, the curriculum and program offerings have been designed to equip students for professional endeavors that are extensions of the work of the Church, echoing the words of Charles Wesley, who wrote:

> My talents, gifts and graces, Lord,
> into Thy blessed hand receive;
> and let me live to preach Thy Word,
> and let me to Thy glory live. ("Give Me the Faith Which Can Remove")

167. An obvious area in which this union of education and calling is seen is in the preparation of ministers. There is a rich tapestry of colleges, universities, and seminaries within the Methodist/Wesleyan tradition that provide quality academic preparation for those who are called into formal leadership roles in a variety of professional ministries. These institutions are vitally important in formulating a body of ministers who are organized around a unifying and distinctive theological and doctrinal tradition within classic Christian orthodoxy.

168. A second area that is equally vital for the propagation of Wesleyan social witness is the preparation of students for professional careers that support compassionate work in society. Many early institutions in the tradition were founded with a particular occupational segment in mind; training for teachers, healthcare workers, social workers, and other helping professions was often at the forefront of institutional founders' minds. The marriage of these professional endeavors with holiness of heart and mind is paramount.

169. Finally, the educational training of all students is fundamentally about aligning their passions and skills to the divine vision of the sanctification of

individual believers and the restoration of all creation. Whether training is based in a primary school, the liberal arts, the sciences, or church ministry, all are aligned with the essential belief that our minds and bodies ultimately belong to the Lord and must be consecrated for his purposes. These students go on to advance the social witness of the Church by the alignment of their intellects and passions with the kingdom of God.

170. Wesleyan higher education is a social witness offering a distinctly Christian academic experience. In many academic contexts, religious beliefs and practices are sidelined or marginalized, making it difficult or impossible to integrate knowledge and faith. Wesleyan colleges and universities provide a public and compelling example of connecting vigorous academic achievement with fervent belief.

171. The Wesleyan vision of holiness also serves as a robust alternative to the self-oriented visions of human flourishing offered in much of the modern academy. Christian holiness doctrine frames an understanding of the human that is aligned with God's revelation and, ultimately, a more healthy and responsible way to live a life of authentic flourishing. Colleges and universities can stake out an academic claim for thinking through the academic disciplines of the humanities and social sciences with the lens of holiness teaching. Colleges and universities can offer scholarship for the sake of the Church and the common good, orienting themselves in service to the broader community as a practical demonstration of holy love, and not simply for the sake of scholarship itself.

Peacemaking

172. Of all the historic characteristics of holy love, perhaps the most important, and most contentious, is peacemaking. Scripture begins in a ruptured relationship: God and humanity, and Cain killing his brother Abel. In Scripture, humanity chooses many ways to reconcile with God and with one another. Fallen humanity establishes cities of refuge, judges as mediators,

and kings, but each human effort falls short in its intended goal. Violence remains normative. The heroes of human history are often great warriors. Indeed, for some, the history of humanity is merely the history of warfare. This glorification of warfare is found throughout religious traditions, including some Christian traditions—despite the fact that, in Scripture, the taking of human life is particularly offensive. Why is it so offensive? It is the destruction of a person created in the very Image of the Creator. It is, at a minimum, a sad reflection on human limitations and our failure to express love for our neighbor.

173. Jesus, on the other hand, is called the Prince of Peace (Isa. 6:6). Peace, however, is not simply the absence of conflict, but the promise of wholeness. It is the restoration of the divine Image in humanity corporately and individually. If peacemaking is the work of the Prince of Peace, it is then also the work of those who follow him. In the words of the apostle Paul, we are called to "the ministry of reconciliation" (2 Cor. 5:18). As people reconciled to our Creator, we are called to the ministry of reconciliation in our families, our communities, our world, and yes, even in the Church itself. We are, Scripture insists, to do unto others as we would do unto ourselves (Matt. 7:12; Luke 6:31). This so-called "golden rule" has profound implications for our ministry as peacemakers. As Christ said, "Blessed are the peacemakers, for they will be called children of God" (Matt. 5:9). For peacemakers are carrying out the ministry of the one who calls us to discipleship.

174. For these reasons, many Christians over the past two thousand years have rejected taking part in warfare, often at great personal cost. Significantly, almost every Christian tradition, even the most vocal of advocates for a "just war" doctrine, have permitted a space for conscientious objectors, honoring the consciences of individuals who have refused military service. Christians remain divided on this issue, but are united in the belief that serving our Lord requires us to work for peace, not merely as the avoidance of conflict, but as a means of the restoration of our full humanity in light of loving God and neighbor.

Health and Wellness

175. As we were created in the Image of God, even our bodies share in the goodness of creation (Gen. 1:31). The physical body has inherent value; it is more than a mere collection of systems and parts. The body is God's gift given to humanity in love in order that humans might pursue God's purpose of sharing his holiness and delighting in his happiness (*TFOD*). Through the gift of our bodies, God calls humanity into a loving relationship first with him and then with one another. When the eternal Son became flesh, he reinforced the holiness of the body and its final purpose. The pursuit of holiness in this life culminates in the resurrection of the body when this mortal and corruptible body shall put on immortality and incorruption (1 Cor. 15:53–54). In relationship with Christ through the Spirit, our bodies participate in the beauty of holiness and receive eternal life through Christ.

176. In this world, holiness must be experienced and expressed through human physicality. By virtue of the natural image, humanity shares physical qualities in relationship with animals and spiritual capacities for relationship with God. As bearers of God's Image, humans also have what John Wesley calls a "political" capacity to serve in the world to fulfill God's intentions (*TFOD*, ¶¶72–73). We fulfill this vocation with God as bearers of the moral image expressed in love for God and neighbor, including the ways our physical bodies incarnate this Image.

177. Throughout human history we have often struggled between two extremes in understanding the nature of the human body. On the one hand, there are those who claim that the physical body is an impediment at best and an outright expression of evil at worst. The body becomes the location of evil and suffering and, therefore, must be transcended in some way. On the other hand, there are those who believe human wholeness is reducible to the physical body. On this view, the body becomes a biological system with no purpose beyond sustaining biological existence on earth. Contrary to both, the teaching of the Church has maintained that because of God's gift of our

bodies, this physical existence has eternal significance. To use more technical language, the creation of persons and of each person has a teleological end (a purpose that draws us). We have an eternal purpose.

178. The physical body is inextricably woven into who the individual is and what that individual will become—both temporally and eternally, both before and after biological death. The life of holiness includes reclaiming God's intention for our physical bodies and the social systems in which we live. We are to be in the world but not of the world (John 17:14–16). It is God's desire that the whole person, body and soul, will flourish in this life and the life to come. Holiness is eternal life being lived out here and now (Rom. 12:1–2).

179. Wesley encouraged this holistic view of holiness and the body through instituted and prudential means of grace and accountability to one another. Through spiritual disciplines such as prayer and reading Scripture, worship and sacraments, and cultivating holy habits, we draw ever closer to God and his purposes. These means of grace open us to the power of the indwelling Holy Spirit and enable us to embrace the divine intention for our flourishing together. They are bodily actions that orient the whole person to God by shaping our hearts for holy living.

180. As we follow God's intention for our health and wellness, we will seek ways to be better stewards of our physical health and well-being. Properly practiced, healthy living is one of the works of piety. It is the spiritual discipline of stewarding the gift of the physical body. Each individual should assume responsibility for her or his own physical well-being as part of our worship of God. This means maintaining a healthy diet, getting sufficient exercise, occasionally fasting, and guarding our bodies from harm. The Christian life lived out physically is not done so with reckless disregard for God's gift of our bodies.

181. John Wesley's most popular book during his lifetime was *Primitive Physick,* a work on self-care that, among other things, contains advice on living a healthy lifestyle. The early Methodists taught people how to improve

and maintain their health. To aid this endeavor, they developed institutions for the provision of healing and ongoing care. We should teach and do the same. Holiness calls us to steward the gift of our physical body. All believers are called to be temples of God both in our bodies and in community in the Church (1 Cor. 3:16; 2 Cor. 6:16).

182. As an expression of love for neighbor, God also calls us to pray for the sick and weak among us (James 5:13–16). This prayer for physical healing is a sign of our love and in no way implies the moral or spiritual inferiority of the infirm. As Jesus noted, people experience the body's frailties and weaknesses for many reasons (John 9:1–3). God's purpose is our final healing through holiness, not necessarily the immediate healing of our bodies. We should always remain focused on eternity as a bulwark against idolizing health and wellness. Each of us will end this physical existence either in death or in the return of Jesus.

183. The works of mercy partly involve ongoing care of the body. This includes healthcare through medical treatment, rehabilitative service, and counseling. These activities and programs help us to flourish within this life. They are also a means of grace in the lives of those who provide care. In service to the needs of "the least of these" (Matt. 25:35–36, 40–45), we participate in the mission of God throughout the world and in our communities. As we serve others in the frailty of physicality, we share in the grace of God.

184. To support the pursuit of holiness through these means of grace, churches should consider the following: training healthcare professionals in their congregations to practice as Christians who offer their skills to those who would not otherwise be served; encouraging healthy habits and exercise as a means of stewardship and responsible witness; providing support for families who care for disabled members; participating in hospice services that maintain the dignity of life in the face of death; providing respite support for families who have someone with ongoing needs; and advocating politically about healthcare issues, to the extent deemed appropriate by the congregation.

185. Since holiness involves "the renewal of God's intention" for the individual, this renewal must include how we treat our bodies. The resurrection of the dead concerns the complete transformation of our bodies, not their loss or abandonment. In the new heaven and earth, we will continue to relate to one another through glorified bodies reflecting the many tribes and tongues of the kingdom (Rev. 21:1, 22–27). The physical body is woven into who we are and what God intends for us in holiness in this world and in the world to come.

186. As the Spirit unites us with Christ in regenerating grace, our bodies are brought into service to Christ. Stewardship of the body is a holy habit. In Christ, we are made members of Christ's body, his new humanity, and we express the holiness of the body of Christ in and through our bodies. In this way, we participate in the new creation and look forward to the consummation of all things when our bodies will finally be healed and holy, healthy, and happy.

Sexuality and Gender Identity

187. God created humanity male and female, and humans thus have the capacity to reflect the beauty of holiness in their relationships with one another and creation. We were made to love and be loved. Given this distinction, honoring God with our bodies demands that we live out holy love in how we relate to ourselves and to others. The second part of the Great Commandment is to "love your neighbor as yourself" (Mark 12:31). Love for neighbor includes holy relationships that govern how we understand our sexuality and our call to be one humanity. God's desire for humans is to reflect his holy nature (Gen. 1:27; Col. 3:9–10) and to live in unbroken intimacy and belonging to him, created as "an act of his perfect love to relate to him in love" (*TFOD*, ¶78).

188. Human sexuality is part of God's gift of our bodies. As such, our relations should reflect the triune relationship of the Father, Son, and Holy Spirit, expressing itself in giving, receiving, and sharing love. As John wrote:

"Whoever does not love does not know God, for God is love" (1 John 4:8). God's love and holiness give us the framework for our sexuality. Humanity exists in community, designed by God from the beginning for relationship with others. The way in which we manifest the Spirit of Christ in and through our lives is, therefore, how we demonstrate God's holiness in us (Matt. 12:33).

189. The association of male and female with the Image of God (Gen. 1:27–28) has its parallel in the equal and complementary relationship of man and woman in the garden (Gen. 2:18–25). God's declaration that male and female together are good finds its expression in God's pronouncement that "It is not good that the man should be alone" (Gen. 2:18a). To remedy this deficiency, God created a woman, as "a helper as his partner" (v. 18b). The term *helper* in Scripture refers to God as well as humans, and it implies no sense of inferiority or subservience. The flourishing of man and woman consisted in their relationship as equal partners in cultivating creation. Full equality in marriage means that God intends the husband and the wife to help one another flourish in holiness.

190. The creation of male and female together suggests balance and harmony rather than hierarchy. While both male and female image God, they are not the same, a difference that begins in the womb. There is balance through a unity in diversity that parallels the harmony between evening and morning, land and sea, and day and night (Gen. 1). The sexual differentiation between man and woman reflects this same harmony and forms part of the order of creation. While the woman was taken from the man (Gen. 2:21–23), man leaves his family and cleaves to woman to complete a circle that points toward their partnership and equality (v. 24). In his teaching on marriage, Jesus affirms this union of one flesh between husband and wife as something "God has joined together" (Mark 10:6–9).

191. The story of Jesus means that God himself has stepped into the human reality, including sexuality. Maleness and femaleness are gifts of God, given to create life, identity, safety, and home. God created gender out of his abundant

goodness. This division into male and female extends beyond sexual activity. We are invited into the life of God and can know him completely as whole persons (1 Cor. 7:3–35). A significant purpose of this marital union is the procreation of children. It is only in the union between male and female that the potential to conceive children can be realized. Couples who choose not to or cannot realize this potential due to forms of infertility do not negate God's design. Some couples may act on this innate desire for children through morally appropriate forms of medical intervention.

192. A second significant purpose of this union is the relationship between the husband and the wife. The sexual differences between a woman and a man are what enable their unification. This is another reason why we believe that marriage is a one-flesh union between two sexually different persons, between a woman and a man in mutual submission to one another.

193. While Jesus indicates that God joins together the husband and the wife, the apostle Paul affirms this principle in referring to marriage as a calling (1 Cor. 7:7, 17). Under the new covenant of Christ, marriage becomes a holy calling that some men and women pursue because God is joining them together. For others, God's call is to celibacy in singleness. The apostle Paul declares: "Let each of you lead the life that the Lord has assigned, to which God called you. This is my rule in all the churches" (v. 17). Marriage and celibacy both enable us to pursue holiness through our bodies and our relationships. They unite in the call to chaste love in friendship that points toward friendship with God and the union of the new humanity in Christ (James 2:21–23).

194. While our sexual activity is part of the goodness of creation, it is not an essential characteristic of full personhood. One dimension of fallenness is the way it alters human sexuality. The sexual act takes on a form of domination in which men and women use one another's bodies solely for pleasure rather than honoring them. They turn one another into objects of pleasure rather than subjects of love. Sin is a power that disorders our desires. In our brokenness, we miss the mark of God's purpose for our lives, including our sexuality.

Though made to be turned outward toward God and one another, reflecting the pure love of God, we have distorted that Image by bending in upon ourselves and reflecting our own wants and desires. And yet, our sexuality is one of many opportunities for all humans to redirect our desires toward godly ends by the power of the Holy Spirit rather than be dominated by them. As Augustine noted, the restlessness of the human heart finds its true home and final peace in the God who has made us for himself (*Confessions*).

195. As a transgression, sin is idolatry. It is choosing to worship something other than God. It is a willful separation from what God had intended, resulting in the corruption of human life and the created order (Rom. 1:18–27; 8:19–23). God's moral law is an expression of his purpose for us and, thus, our flourishing. When we transgress God's purpose, we abuse the gifts of God (Gen. 3:1–7). Even our love for one another becomes corrupt when we fail to realize God's design in our decisions. We replace the other-oriented, self-giving nature of love with a bondage to a self-consumed heart (*TFOD*, ¶81).

196. When we fail to realize God's purpose for our lives as sexual beings, we must repent and receive the power of new life through the Holy Spirit. Prevenient grace is given to enable every person to turn from sin and repent. Confession involves speaking the truth about ourselves while repentance is turning back to God and entrusting our entire life to his care. Jesus tells us when that happens, we are "born from above" (John 3:3). God's life is imparted into ours. Humans are brought into the life of God. This is a family relationship of mutual knowing and belonging to God. It is not merely imitation or imputation but is participation in his life (John 13:8; Rom. 1:6; 8:1; Gal. 5:24). Salvation involves the healing of our brokenness and the perfection of God's purpose for us through the restoration of intimacy with God and the freedom to live for one another in holy love.

197. The newness of life found through faith in Jesus Christ and the power of the Spirit incorporates our whole person. Christ does not leave us powerless over our sexual drives. He begins the restoration process to recreate

our broken sexual desires into his purpose. He brings us into a new family, the Church, in which we can participate in holy friendship and reshape our desires and affections. Every sector of our lives can be restored when we are born again by the Spirit and cooperate with the work of the Spirit in our lives.

198. Jesus invites us through the sacrifice of his own life into a God-centered way of living, loving, and relating. Through Christ's atoning death, the holiness of God and all of our sins, including our sexual sins, meet. When Jesus took our sinful human nature into himself, he took every element of rebellion and the resultant brokenness of our sexuality. He has taken our sin from us in his self-giving (1 Peter 4:1–2). As redeemed humanity, we are then commanded and enabled to become in practice what we are in Christ Jesus—dead to sin and alive to God (Rom. 6:5–8).

199. The sanctification of our sexuality involves yielding ourselves fully to Christ. The Spirit can cleanse the yielded heart, transforming our affections and desires by filling us with perfect love (2 Cor. 5:14–15). He can help us in every sexual temptation (1 Cor. 10:13). Regardless of our claims about our sexuality, no one is condemned to be a servant of sin. The Holy Spirit's sanctifying grace empowers us with the love to live fully as God desires. We can experience being satisfied in God's love (Ps. 63:1–8; 90:14). Our task as followers of Christ is to proclaim this saving truth to the world, even regarding our sexuality.

Race and Ethnicity

200. God created humanity to be in community. Human communities have differences between them, but in God's design these differences should not lead to divisions or create destructive hierarchies. Relationships between human persons should mirror the unity in diversity found in the loving relations of the Father, Son, and Holy Spirit. Expanding the family, tribe, and nation, these differences in humanity should be celebrated. Throughout Scripture they appear in forms of ethnic, cultural, and geographical particularities as humanity came to occupy God's creation. As believers increasingly

embody God's holiness, we will see the beauty in the astounding diversity of his creation, including the ethnic and cultural diversity of human communities.

201. In this fallen world, however, the beauty of the ethnic and cultural diversity of the human family itself becomes a source of great brokenness and pain. The Scripture does not divide humanity into races even in its acknowledgment of ethnic diversity (Gen. 10). The conflicts between Jews and Gentiles experienced in early Christianity emerged from religious and cultural differences among peoples and nations, not race (Gal. 3:28). The call to holiness compels believers to seek the good of others, whereas the disgrace of racism in the human family is a sign of the brokenness and division of our world. Humans ultimately cannot flourish as they should when racism is present.

202. Even though scriptural writers used descriptions such as Cushite and Ethiopian to differentiate peoples, the scope of the biblical story suggests that these differences remained within a common descent rooted in the Image of God. God's plan and purpose for creation includes all nations, tribes, and tongues without consideration of people's physical appearance. Within Scripture, the grace of God extends to all because all humanity was created in the Image of God, Christ died for all, and the Spirit's prevenient grace beckons all persons toward redemption in Christ. For this reason, early Christianity was a multicultural and multiethnic reality.

203. Within Scripture, the land plays an important role in shaping and being shaped by humanity. Ethnic and cultural diversity partly stems from this relationship with the land, giving rise to the rich diversity of human existence. This diversity is not abrogated in the new creation but enhanced through the formation of a new heaven and a new earth. The biblical identity of the people of God is not a uniformity but rather a unity that preserves all tribes and tongues. The original divine intention remains that one humanity evolves into a rich diversity that does not compromise the common human nature. In this way, ethnic and cultural distinctions reflect God's triune nature of unity in diversity.

204. Geographical distinction means that people share customs, traditions, and practices based on the physical places they inhabit and the ways in which various regions shape them. These geographical locations can relate to some ethnic and cultural particularities, while transcending others. Local art and music express their own region while gesturing beyond themselves to a deeper beauty.

205. Cultural distinctions emerge in conversation with geography. As people inhabit the land, they express God's creativity through distinct knowledge, beliefs, values, arts, symbols, and even tools for living that distinguish them from other peoples in the world.

206. Ethnic distinctions mean some communities hold in common various affinities or characteristics. These may be related to lineage or descent such as in a tribe, clan, or family, and they carry forward a strong bond. People can also have a shared political or covenantal history. Many communities have shared languages and cultural expressions that bind them together.

207. Although these distinctions should be celebrated, they have at times led to forms of tribalism in which loyalty to one's group has prompted demonization of outsiders. Human history is replete with examples of one group seeking to do enormous harm to another group even within the same geographical borders. Despite Christ's call for the Church to be a new humanity, Christians have sometimes participated in forms of violence in the name of a particular identity. Jesus's words remind us that it should "not be so among you; but whoever wishes to be great among you must be your servant" (Matt. 20:26).

208. While Scripture includes the distinctions outlined above as well as the temptation to tribalism, the category of race was constructed by human beings based upon perceived differences related to skin color and physical characteristics in order to obtain or maintain social power and dominance. These perceived differences have led to a faulty hierarchy of races in which some ethnic groups are viewed as inferior and, therefore, subjected to forms

of segregation and subjugation. Race adds a new element to tribalism that intensifies and expands it.

209. In the modern period, false interpretations of Scripture have been combined with pseudoscientific theories to construct egregious beliefs and practices of prejudice that dehumanize and destroy human lives. Some societies have codified such prejudice into law to justify the development of massive, long-standing systems of oppression such as the slave trade in Africa and the transatlantic slave trade. These systems displaced millions of Africans by forcibly removing them from their homeland and ensuring the cruel enslavement of Africans and their children.

210. As the people of God turned to follow the practices of surrounding cultures, acceptance of caste and class systems compromised the commitment to love one's neighbor as oneself. This has been evident in prejudices across groups, racialization, and racism. The deeply entrenched nature of race prejudice has led many Christians to participate in creating, defending, and propagating these ungodly systems.

211. John Wesley spoke passionately against the practice of slavery in his day by appealing to the need for all believers to seek the good of the other through holiness of heart: "Are you *a man?* Then you should have a *human* heart. But have you indeed? What is your heart made of? Is there no such principle as compassion there? Do you never *feel* another's pain? Have you no sympathy? No sense of human woe? No pity for the miserable?" (*Thoughts Upon Slavery,* italics original). By appealing to the need to order the affections in compassion and sympathy for our fellow human beings, Wesley pointed toward the way the Spirit begins to restore the human conscience in holiness.

212. As Christians walk in the way of holiness through the Spirit's regenerating and sanctifying grace, we must reject all forms of race prejudice and the dehumanizing theories and consequent economic, political, and ecclesiastical or organizational practices they inspire. As the holiness preacher Martin

Wells Knapp declared: "barriers of race, and color, and social position have no true place in Christ's Church" (*Lightning Bolts from Pentecostal Skies*). God calls us to spread scriptural holiness, empowered by the Spirit, to root out prejudice and racism in the heart, the home, the Church, and the world. To be entirely sanctified is to live in perfect love and to drive out hatred, jealously, greed, and any other disordered affection that causes us to devalue our neighbor (*TFOD*, ¶¶130–33).

213. The Church should embody the biblical ideal of the people of God as a "priestly kingdom and a holy nation" (Ex. 19:6). With the coming of Jesus, that ideal supersedes distinctions between Jew and Gentile in the newly envisioned "chosen race" created and descended from God—"God's own people"—in order that we may proclaim the mighty acts of him who called us out of darkness into his marvelous light (1 Peter 2:9). The second-century bishop Polycarp of Smyrna saw himself as a member of "the God-loving and God-fearing race of Christians" (*Martyrdom of Polycarp*). As believers in this new humanity of the Church, we should celebrate ethnic diversity as part of the beauty of God's creation and the coming together of all tribes and tongues in the new creation.

214. The gospel of the kingdom is the triune God's decisive word of liberation for the whole creation revealed in the life, ministry, death, burial, resurrection, ascension, and promised return of Jesus of Nazareth. We are called to proclaim in word and deed the new temple God is building out of living stones from all nations. In those contexts where prejudice prevails or racism remains, we spread scriptural holiness by living out the multicultural and multiethnic reality of the kingdom. We also engage in works of mercy toward our neighbors so that they may see the love of Christ in our lives. This requires us to uphold the dignity of every human person in the face of inhumanity and to cooperate with the Spirit's prevenient work of stirring the conscience through political and social engagement for justice.

215. Since salvation broadly construed encompasses "the dawn of grace in the soul to its consummation in glory" (John Wesley, "The Scripture Way of

Salvation"), it includes the social, political, individual, and spiritual dimensions of created reality. Like the message of Joseph and Moses before Pharaoh; and of Peter, Stephen, and Paul before religious and political leaders; and even Jesus himself, announcing the good news of God's reign includes preaching liberation to the oppressed alongside justification by grace through faith alone (Eph. 2:8–9). Like the daughters of Zelophehad before the Israelite community, the gospel compels the whole Church to engage in social and political action (Num. 36:1–4). Like the songs of Miriam and of Mary, the good news results in both evangelism and mission (Ex. 15:21; Luke 1:46–55).

CONCLUSION

The Promise of Holiness

216. In Matthew 5:48 Jesus proclaims in his Sermon on the Mount the striking words, "Be perfect, therefore, as your heavenly Father is perfect." This is the last verse in the chapter and it's not easy to miss. At the beginning of chapter 5 we read the famous Beatitudes: "Blessed are the poor in spirit, for theirs is the kingdom of heaven. Blessed are those who mourn, for they will be comforted. . . . Blessed are those who hunger and thirst for righteousness, for they will be filled. . . . Blessed are the pure in heart, for they will see God. . . ." (vv. 3–8). In John Wesley's translation of these texts he doesn't use the word *blessed* but, instead, he uses the word *happy*. And he's not the only one to have taken this approach to the translation of these verses.

217. To understand his choice, however, it is good to understand what he meant by the term *happy*. It was not a simple feeling or sense of elation, however nice that experience of happiness can be. Wesley was an Oxford man through and through, and so he studied Aristotle and virtue ethics. Happiness in this tradition is much closer to contentment, fulfillment, and completeness. It is to be what one was meant to be from the beginning. And so Wesley saw Matthew 5 as beginning with the description of the happy life that God has for us—the complete life—culminating in that wonderful command (and, therefore, promise) to "be perfect . . . as [our] heavenly Father is perfect" (Matt. 5:48). This is what Wesley said in his *Explanatory Notes Upon the New Testament*:

> *Therefore ye shall be perfect, as your Father who is in heaven is perfect*—So the original runs, referring to all that holiness which is described in the foregoing verses, which our Lord in the beginning of the chapter recommends as happiness, and in the close of it as perfection. And how wise and gracious is this, to sum up, and as it were seal, all His commandments

> with a promise, even the proper promise of the gospel, that He will "put" these "laws in our minds, and write them in our hearts"! He well knew how ready our unbelief would be to cry out, This is impossible! and therefore stakes upon it all the power, truth, and faithfulness of Him to whom all things are possible. (italics original)

The life that God intends for each and every one of us is a life of true contentment, wholeness, and happiness. And he commands us to seek it (therefore, it is a promise) not for any other reason than our healing and, therefore, our freedom.

218. Sin has had the effect that it has left humanity, society, and the world itself corrupted and disordered, lacking this happiness and freedom. We know this sin all too well. And yet Christ's life, death, and resurrection have overcome sin, death, and hell. But many believers have not been told that this victory is something that can be experienced now, a reality in which believers are made free in this life. A Wesleyan view of salvation is that eternal life begins not with death, but even at the moment we first respond to God's grace, his light and life becoming our own. In response to this grace, this empowerment from God, we are convicted of our sins, enabled to repent, and are given his pardon, being justified. As those pardoned by God, we experience a new life. This life is more than a change of status with God; it is a *real* change in which we are born anew. And when we have that new life—regeneration—we will enter a period of growth in Christ, fueled by the Spirit, that ultimately leads to the promised perfection of the Father.

219. The hope that we have is that God can make us whole at any moment. And he has the power to do just that. The God who made the heavens and the earth can change you and me. But his usual way of working with us is through free grace (those experiences of grace that belong to God alone, such as the moment of new birth, justification, or entire sanctification) and through cooperant grace (the empowered growth that results from cooperating with or responding to God's initiative, the transforming walk with Christ).

220. And God has given us grace—he gives more grace than we can ever imagine—and also the means of grace, channels of his grace. The means are opportunities of encounter. God has said that he would meet us in these ways, and so we run to meet him there. The means are many but are generally understood to be within two categories: acts of piety and works of mercy. Means of grace are, as John Wesley said in his sermon by that title, means not ends. The end is a life of wholeness made possible by a dynamic relationship with God. The means engage the end. Among the acts of piety are meditating on Scripture, fasting, and prayer. The primary channel—or "grand channel," as Wesley called it—is Holy Communion, when by faith we partake of the body and blood of Christ, being filled with his life through this means. The works of mercy are acts of mercy including clothing the naked, feeding the hungry, or visiting the sick. In these acts of kindness, God's grace overflows and it changes us. The means should be understood as a pattern of the Christian life, one marked by growth in Christlikeness, empowered by the Spirit. They also remind us that the life of holiness is not one that can be lived in isolation. John Wesley famously said, "there is no holiness, but social holiness" (*Hymns and Sacred Poems*), and by that he meant that we couldn't be holy apart from others helping us, and we helping them. Holiness is a communal experience.

221. As such, holiness is not meant for the individual alone but as part of God's work to renew the whole creation. One of the hallmarks of a Wesleyan perspective is that God's work in us individually doesn't end with us; that work spreads as we cooperate with God's work in the world. His act of setting us free from the power and dominion of sin reverberates like ripples in a pond as that freedom means that we can be about his work.

222. The life of holiness, this walk with Christ and with our fellow Christians, is marked by process and instantaneous moments. The balance is essential. There are distinct moments—free grace—when God moves in us to make us whole, such as the new birth and entire sanctification. Yet the process, the walk, takes place both before and after every moment of transformation. And after the new birth, the importance of our cooperation increases as we both

rely on the means of grace to walk with Christ and also commit ourselves to good works that lead to the freedom of sanctification. The point is our renewal, to actually become the persons God created us to be, to live in societies as he intended them to be and prepare ourselves for the new creation in which even the created order will be set right according to God's purposes.

223. So why are the faithful called blessed, or happy, in Matthew 5? The answer is that they're holy; they're now, by the very power of God, living the life that is true contentment, wholeness, and happiness. Sin—always foreign to humanity's true life—no longer has power over them. They're free. The chains that once bound them have fallen off; their lives are driven by holy love. What the Beatitudes describe is actually what holiness looks like.

224. The blessed, or happy, will be part of the kingdom of God; they will enjoy his very presence. They will receive comfort, true comfort, often described as "peace . . . which surpasses all understanding" (Phil. 4:7). They will inherit the earth, the creation as God had intended it to be from the beginning. They will be filled, even with the very life of God. They will receive mercy, both God's merciful forgiveness but also the mercy to live the lives they were always intended to live. They "will be called children of God" (Matt. 5:9), because that is what they are—their spirits answering the Spirit's word and crying, "Abba, Father" (Gal. 4:6–7; Rom. 8:15). In other words, they will be like Christ. This is the beautiful promise of holiness.

> May the God of peace himself sanctify you entirely; and may your spirit and soul and body be kept blameless at the coming of our Lord Jesus Christ. The one who calls you is faithful, and he will do this. (1 Thess. 5:23–24)

APPENDIX: STUDY AND GROUP DISCUSSION QUESTIONS

Chapter One: The Holy Trinity: Ground of Holiness

1. When you think about holiness, do you usually begin with God or with people? Were you surprised that the book began its exploration of holiness with God?

2. God's very character is described as "holy," making him unique, like none other. How does his holiness, or his character, point us to a holy life? How can we reflect him when he is like nothing else that we know?

3. We can't speak about God's holiness apart from his love. He is love. How does his love correspond to the description of God's uniqueness, or even separateness, from the created world and us?

4. What does it look like in our own lives to live according to God's holy love, the love that is self-giving by its very nature?

5. What does it mean in our walk with God to speak of evil as something that doesn't in itself exist, but is, in reality, a lack of holiness or of the good?

6. How is pride contrary to holiness?
7. Have you ever thought of holiness as a continuation, and restoration, of the Son's work in creation? What might that mean in our daily lives?
8. At Jesus's baptism the Spirit descended on him as the Father proclaimed him "my Son." He didn't need baptism like we do, but we receive the same Spirit in our baptism. How has your baptism played a role in your walk with Christ?
9. Jesus is described in the text as having "contagious holiness." How does that strike you?
10. What does it mean that the blood of Christ sanctifies us?
11. In what ways does the work of Christ and the work of the Holy Spirit act together for our sanctification?
12. What are characteristics of the life made possible by the Spirit's active work in our lives?
13. How does Origen's description of Jesus's parable of the new and old wine-skins help you to see the life of holiness more clearly from that text?
14. How does the Spirit's work of love unite us to God and to one another?
15. What means do we have to encounter the life-giving work of the Holy Spirit in our own lives?

Chapter Two: Scriptural Holiness: Command and Promise

1. How is it that being saved and living a good life are connected?
2. How does reading the commands of God in Scripture as "covered promises" help us to better understand God's will in Scripture?
3. Instead of looking at the Bible as a "repository of information," we are encouraged to view it as "the terrain of divine encounter." How does this change, or enhance, your view of Scripture?
4. In the Old Testament we can see God's plan of restoration unfold the moment the fall takes place. Part of his plan was to create a holy people who would reflect his very life. In what way does Israel's calling set a pattern for holy living today?
5. Love of God and love of neighbor go together. How can we see this in the Old Testament law?
6. Being a holy people means being holy as God is holy. And it comes with community expectations. The text lists some of the ways that this can be seen in the Old Testament. What might be other examples of how we show God's love to one another in our own communities?
7. Idolatry and injustice hindered the call of Israel. Both can sometimes be seen clearly (worshipping an idol, for example), but at other times they are less easily identified. How does the story of Israel help us today to see idolatry and injustice in all of its forms, whether clear or not? And how might that help us to avoid them?
8. Holiness has sometimes been confused as a list of rules. How does understanding holiness as "an issue of the heart" help to avoid this approach?
9. In Jesus Christ we have the very pattern of holiness, in human form. How does his life shape your own view of holiness?
10. How does Jesus's death and resurrection make holiness possible? How, in other words, is his sacrifice and victory applied to us?

11. With Christ as the pattern and means of holiness, how do Paul's letters help us better understand the life of holiness? What examples can we find in them?
12. What does it mean to be "in Christ"?
13. Have you ever considered the connection between holiness and the new creation? How does this ultimate vision shape your view of holiness lived now?

Chapter Three: The Triumph of Grace

1. What is holy love and how is it different from other loves?
2. How does God's holy love—exemplified in the life, death, and resurrection of Christ—reveal his universal offer of salvation?
3. How does the Church carry on Israel's calling to be a holy people set apart?
4. The new birth was a central theme of the Evangelical Revival and can be seen in John 3. What transforming role does the new birth play in leading us from a life of sin to a life of holy love?
5. What is assurance and what role does it play in the Christian life?
6. What does it mean that the new birth produces not just habits in our lives, but transformed affections or holy desires?
7. What do you think of the idea of "spiritual respiration," that God continuously breathes life and grace in our souls and we respond with prayer and praise?
8. The life of holiness includes moments of transformation and seasons of growth. What does it mean to grow into the holy life? How is this growth made possible?
9. Although it's used in Scripture, the word *perfect* confuses some Christians. How are we to understand the perfection that God calls us to in entire sanctification?
10. What are the marks of an entirely sanctified life?
11. When we come to know that entire sanctification is something that God wants for us *in this life,* how does this change your view of God's promises?
12. Holiness in the present is a signpost of glorification, the full and complete goal of the process of salvation. How does this longer view help us to both appreciate the need for holiness in our lives today, but also encourage us in our walk with Christ?

Chapter Four: Holiness and the Church: Social Holiness

1. Which of the means of grace have you found most beneficial in your walk with Christ?
2. Sometimes grace has been described as divine favor or mercy, but in the Wesleyan tradition it is much more dynamic—it's the power of God. How does this change your view of grace and its role in your life?
3. The means of grace impact us personally, but also corporately as we practice them together. How is your local church designed to encourage participation in the means of grace?
4. How do the different categories of means of grace help you to understand them and their place in the Christian life?
5. Holiness and worship cannot be separated. How has worship played a vital role in your walk of faith?
6. When we speak of worship as "the defining act of the gathered Church" and joining "in the eternal gathering of heaven," how does that change your view of worship?
7. Baptism is one of the two sacraments given by Christ himself and a means by which God works to cleanse us and make us a part of his body. What does it mean for the Church's life that we are all united in God's work through the waters of baptism?
8. Baptism is God's work and can only be performed once in a person's life. Why has the Church (since the time of Christ) taught that this sacrament is unrepeatable?
9. Knowing that the Eucharist, or Holy Communion, is much more than remembering what Jesus did in the past, but actually encountering him now, how is the Eucharist vital in your own life? And do you participate in it as much as you'd like?
10. The Eucharist is a meal where past, present, and future collide. How does this shape your understanding of this holy meal?

11. Singing the faith is a means of grace. What hymns or spiritual songs have touched you most over the course of your life? Which one of Charles Wesley's hymns would you say has impacted you most?
12. When was the last time that you heard, or even preached, a sermon on holiness that moved you, calling you closer to the love of God?
13. When have you experienced another believer "watching over [you] in love" and how did it help you in your walk with Christ?
14. What opportunities for "watching over one another in love" does your church have as a part of its corporate life?

Chapter Five: Holiness in Practice: The Church's Witness

1. Thinking about the story of Jonah, who might be the "Ninevites" in our world today? Do we harbor such ill will toward them that we don't want them to know the love of God?

2. Holiness is described as "not the absence of faults but the presence of perfect love—a love that encompasses both God and neighbor." How does this help us to understand the nature of holiness and how to avoid making it, and our love for others, into some sort of checklist?

3. The chapter includes a very helpful description of social interaction based on holiness:

   > This call is lived out in a trifold expression that is demonstrated through: (1) *being*—our individual and/or communal dispositions; (2) *doing*—the tangible acts that we perform and omissions we opt to make; and (3) *becoming*—the inner transformation that takes place in our lives as we continually draw closer to God and live in harmony with his children, our neighbors.

   How does this help you to appreciate (or even act upon) the corporate nature of God's call to wholeness in Christ?

4. How does John Wesley's view of poverty alter your own thoughts on the topic?

5. Have you ever thought of engaging the poor in our communities as a means of grace for them and for you?

6. We all experience some form of poverty, whether material, spiritual, or social. How does this realization help us not to think of the poor as simply "the other"?

7. Education has sometimes been thought of as preparation for professional endeavors or to learn new ideas, but how would our vision of education change if we insisted that it make us better disciples of Jesus Christ? What would be the Church's role in making this possible?

8. As Christ is both the Prince of Peace and the embodiment of a holy life, how does he shape our view of peacemaking and its place in our lives?
9. Holiness is something lived out, meaning that it involves our bodies. And bodies are good, a gift even. In what ways do we embody the call to holiness, both in what we do and what we refrain from doing bodily?
10. As a gift, and an intrinsic part of us, how can we view care of our bodies as an answer to the call to holiness?
11. Sexuality is a gift from God, but often an area where many struggle. Given that we are created to reflect the holy love of God, how does this truth shape a right view of sex and sexual relations?
12. The creation of male and female in the biblical narrative indicates balance rather than hierarchy. How can men and women strive to create communities of balance together as an expression of God's intention for creation?
13. How can the Church be organized such that it supports both the call to marriage and the call to singleness?
14. Unity in diversity is inherent to God as Trinity and to humanity (family, tribe, and nation). How does the call to holiness help us to see the beauty of God's diverse creation?
15. Racism is a sign of brokenness. As people called to holiness, or wholeness, what are some ways that you and your community can work to overcome racism?
16. While distinctions exist culturally and otherwise, how can the call to holiness help us to overcome the dangers of tribalism while seeing the goodness of cultural uniqueness?

Conclusion: The Promise of Holiness

1. How does John Wesley's understanding of "happiness" and "perfection" help us to better understand Jesus's Sermon on the Mount in Matthew 5?
2. How do the concepts of "free grace" and "cooperant grace" enable us to see the holy life more clearly, both God's work in us and our work with him?
3. John Wesley's statement, "there is no holiness, but social holiness," means that we need one another to live a holy life. It also indicates that we need the means of grace found in Christian community. How is the both/and, individual/corporate approach to holiness lived out in your own church community?
4. To see holiness as "true contentment, wholeness, and happiness" or as a life that looks like Christ himself is to emphasize the freedom that grace makes possible in our lives. In what ways has this study inspired you to seek that grace and the promise of holiness available to each and every one of us?

ABOUT THE EDITOR

Ryan N. Danker (ThD, Boston University) is the founding director of the John Wesley Institute in Washington, DC. A scholar of modern church history, particularly the Evangelical Revival and the Wesley brothers, he served for many years on the faculties of Greensboro College and Wesley Theological Seminary and has taught at Asbury Theological Seminary, Trinity Anglican Seminary, and Virginia Theological Seminary. He is the president of the Charles Wesley Society, an editor of *Firebrand Magazine*, and serves on the Foundation of the The Living Church.

Printed by Libri Plureos GmbH in Hamburg,
Germany

9 798888 001813